BUILDING PEACE,
SEEKING JUSTICE

A Population-Based Survey on Attitudes about
Accountability and Social Reconstruction in the
Central African Republic

JULY 2010

PATRICK VINCK | PHUONG PHAM

**HUMAN
RIGHTS
CENTER**
UNIVERSITY
OF
CALIFORNIA
BERKELEY

CONTENTS

EXECUTIVE SUMMARY

DECADES OF POLITICAL INSTABILITY, state fragility, mismanagement, and a series of armed conflicts have led the Central African Republic (CAR) to a state of widespread violence and poverty. This study provides a better understanding of the scope and magnitude of violence in CAR and its consequences, as well as a snapshot of what the citizens of CAR believe is the best way to restore peace. It also examines the issue of justice and accountability for the serious crimes that were committed.

This report provides the findings from a survey of 1,879 adults, residents of CAR, randomly selected in the capital city of Bangui, and the prefectures of Lobaye, Ombella M'Poko, Ouham, and Ouham Pende. These prefectures encompass a large geographic area representing 52 percent of the total population of CAR and have experienced varying levels of exposure to the conflicts. Locally trained teams conducted the interviews between November and December 2009.

This report provides a detailed analysis of results on a wide range of topics related to the population's priorities and needs, exposure to violence, security, community cohesion and engagement, access to information, conflict resolution, reintegration of former combatants, transitional justice, and reparations for victims. Interviewers used an open-ended format and respondents could provide more than one answer to most questions.

Highlights of the survey's findings are as follows:

Building Peace:

- Peace, defined by respondents as the absence of violence and freedom from fear, is the main priority, followed by concerns over livelihood activities (work) and money. The lack of security was highlighted even in daily activities: more than one in four respondents reported feeling unsafe while walking or sleeping at night, going to the nearest village, or meeting strangers. When asked who provides them with security, more than half the respondents (54%) mention God, while 3 percent mentioned the police/*gendarmes*. Given the current dynamic of the conflict, the sense of insecurity was highest in the northern prefectures of Ouham and Ouham Pende. However, many respondents also reported feeling unsafe in Bangui.

- The population has been exposed to widespread violence and human rights abuses.

  - Four out of five respondents said they had to flee their home at some point during the various conflicts since 2002.

  - About three out of five had goods or property stolen or destroyed, were separated from household members, or thought their lives were threatened.

Many respondents were also directly exposed to violence:

  - Twenty percent said they had been beaten or physically attacked.

  - Ten percent said they had been abducted (5% for at least a week).

  - Fourteen percent said armed groups forced them to work; 5 percent were forced to loot, 2 percent to beat someone, and 1 percent to kill someone.

  - Over 10 percent of the respondents in the prefectures of Ouham and Ouham Pende reported having witnessed pillaging and beating, having been forced to flee their home or village, having property stolen or destroyed, and being threatened with death over the last 12 months.

  - Twenty-one percent of all respondents reported witnessing acts of sexual violence by armed groups.

  - Six percent of the women surveyed reported an experience of sexual violence committed by armed groups, and 6 percent reported sexual violence committed by perpetrators other than armed groups. Sexual violence was most frequently reported by women in Ouham Pende (14%), a rate comparable to that found in the eastern Democratic Republic of Congo.[1]

- In addition to conflict-related violence, domestic violence is pervasive: 22 percent of the women report having been physically beaten by a household member, most frequently for disobeying or arguing.

- Most respondents (61%) identify the root cause of the conflict as the struggle for power between political elites. Reflecting the notion that this is predominantly a political conflict, most respondents believe peace must be achieved through dialogue (56%) or by having elections (23%). However, there was some pessimism as to whether peace can be achieved; only half the respondents believed it is possible to live in peace in CAR (54%) and with neighboring countries

---

1 Vinck P, Pham PN, Baldo S, Shigekane R. *Living with Fear: A Population-Based Survey on Attitudes about Peace, Justice and Social Reconstruction in Eastern Congo.* Human Rights Center, University of California, Berkeley; Payson Center for International Development, Tulane University; International Center for Transitional Justice, New York; 2008.

(50%). One in four did not believe it was possible to have peace. Respondents in the northern prefectures were more likely to be pessimistic about prospects for a lasting peace.

- Twenty-three percent of respondents said having free and fair elections was a means for a durable peace. A large majority (94%) said they plan to vote in the next presidential elections, and most felt confident that they would be able to vote freely.

- Respondents expressed high expectations that Disarmament, Demobilization, and Reintegration (DDR) programs would contribute to a lasting peace.

- Three out of four respondents felt uncomfortable interacting with former combatants in the following contexts: sharing a drink or living as neighbors or in the same household.

- A quarter of respondents felt they knew nothing or very little about events in CAR and 41 percent said they never listened to the radio, the most common source of information in the country.

Seeking Justice:

- The vast majority of respondents (98%) said those responsible for the violence should be held accountable. Respondents identified murder (91%), theft and destruction of property (66%), and sexual violence (52%) as the principal crimes committed by combatants. Respondents provided a long list of individuals or groups that should be held accountable, including current and former presidents, and leaders of rebel groups. When asked what should happen to those responsible for the violence, 46 percent said they should confront justice, 27 percent said they should go to jail, 21 percent said they should be killed with or without judicial proceedings, and 19 percent said they should be punished.

- When provided with four options for prosecuting those responsible for the violence, over half of the respondents (52%) said they should be tried in the national courts while 27 percent said they should be tried in CAR by an international court. Fourteen percent preferred international trials outside of the country, while 7 percent preferred no trials at all. Thus, in general, respondents clearly prefer trials conducted in CAR. However, only one third of respondents perceived the quality of the judicial system as good or very good. These findings are consistent with those found in other post-conflict settings where the population wants justice to be proximate to the conflict in order to witness and participate in the process.

- One third of respondents have heard of the International Criminal Court, with figures by prefectures ranging from 7 percent in Ouham to 63 percent in Bangui. In general, the perception of the Court is positive, with most respondents expecting a positive impact, such as bringing justice, and helping prevent crimes.

- When asked who the victims of the various armed conflicts are, respondents gave the following definitions: the civilian population (75%), women (54%), children (46%), and the elderly (25%). When asked what should be done for the victims, they said restitution (60%), followed by money (34%). About half the respondents said reparation should be both individual and communal, while 20 percent said it should be only individual.

- It is important to respondents to know the truth about what happened during the conflicts, and why it happened. Most (74%) also believe memorials are important.

These results should be instructive to the Government of the Central African Republic, nongovernmental organizations, and other agencies as they develop policies to address the legacy of armed conflict in CAR. They are also a reminder that consulting the population and deepening our understanding of war-affected communities is essential to build a lasting peace.

The key recommendations to emerge from this study are:

To the CAR Government and Armed Groups:

- Work together to implement the goals of the Inclusive Political Dialogue, including the effective disarmament, demobilization, and reintegration of combatants back into society and hold free and fair presidential elections. The citizens of CAR view combatant reintegration programs and elections as integral steps for building a lasting peace.

- Stop preying on the population and collecting illegal taxes at road blocks. These tactics instill fear among the population and hinder their ability to carry on with their daily lives.

To the CAR Government:

- Reform the security sector and remove perpetrators of serious crimes from their positions. The police and *gendarmes* must be trained and supported to fulfill their mandate of protecting—not preying on—civilians.

- Bring those responsible for violations of human rights and international humanitarian law to justice. The government should support the judiciary to ensure that courts can operate independently and fairly. This will help raise public confidence in the judiciary and supporting the rule of law.

- Prioritize the provision of basic services, including education, health care, and transportation (e.g., the road network).

To the Civil Society and the International Community:

- Pressure the government, political parties, and armed groups to ensure that elections and DDR processes are effectively implemented in a transparent, free, and fair manner.

- Provide sufficient financial and technical support to the electoral process to guarantee free and fair elections and ensure a peaceful transition.

- Work with the government to rebuild infrastructure and services and uphold the rule of law. The focus on humanitarian needs in the north should not prevent investment to address structural and chronic poverty in all of CAR. Respondents identified peace, employment, and basic services as priorities. If any of these are neglected, political and physical stability will be hard to establish and sustain.

- Engage with the population to address domestic violence and other forms of violence at the community level

- Continue to document violations of human rights and international humanitarian law and press for accountability. The international community should continue to support civil society in its efforts to document human rights abuses and assist victims. The international community should also maintain a UN peacekeeping mission in CAR for the foreseeable future. Its presence will help guarantee a certain level of stability and allow for the completion of DDR, elections, and reform of the security sector.

- Work to develop a regional security strategy to address cross-border issues and lawless border zones.

To the International Criminal Court:

- Increase public information and outreach activities, especially in the interior of the country. The proportion of respondents who are aware of the ICC was relatively high, but there is still a great need to target groups with little or no access to media.

- Reconsider holding *in situ* proceedings in CAR, security permitting. The survey found strong support for local trials.

- Broaden the scope of investigations to include serious crimes committed throughout the country, especially in the North.

- Work with national institutions to ensure that the investigations contribute to establishing a historical record of events in CAR.

INTRODUCTION

MANY COUNTRIES AROUND THE WORLD are locked in a cycle of poverty, conflict, and destruction. Few, however, have received as little attention as the Central African Republic (CAR). Since its independence from France in 1960, CAR has been embroiled in successive military coup attempts and violent power transitions, leaving the country fragmented, underdeveloped, and violent.[2] The government has had little control outside of the capital Bangui, and instability has been aggravated by warlords, rebels, and mercenaries, who freely use remote rural areas as bases for their operations.[3] Several peacekeeping forces and investigations by the International Criminal Court into serious crimes allegedly committed in CAR have made international news, but the situation remains relatively unknown, especially compared to conflicts in neighboring Darfur and Democratic Republic of Congo. Yet, this is a critical time for CAR. Conflicts in Darfur and the presence of the Lord's Resistance Army in the southeast of the country highlight the need for a regional approach to security. Internally, the country faces challenges to address the presence of several armed groups, hold presidential elections, and disarm, demobilize, and reintegrate former combatants. This study provides details regarding the scope and magnitude of violence in CAR and its consequences, as well as a snapshot of what the citizens of CAR believe is the best way to restore peace and rebuild their country. The goal is to inform the development of policies that will affect survivors' individual and collective lives for years to come.

Short Background to the Conflict and Involvement of the ICC

The political situation in CAR has been unstable since its independence from France in 1960, marked by four coups d'état and many more failed attempts.[4] The most recent coup occurred in 2003 when Francois Bozizé seized power from Ange-Félix Patassé. Patassé had won multi-party presidential elections in 1993. His presidency, however, was marked by a series of military coup attempts prompting

---

2   International Crisis Group. *Africa Briefing N° 69: Central African Republic: Keeping the Dialogue Alive. Nairobi/Brussels*: ICG, 2010; Berman EG, Lombard LN *The Central African Republic and Small Arms*. Geneva: Small Arms Survey, 2008.
3   International Crisis Group. *Africa Report N°136: Central African Republic: Anatomy of a Phantom State. Nairobi/Brussels*: ICG, 2007.
4   Berman, EG et al.

the involvement of a small UN force. In 1999, Patassé was reelected but failed to unite the various armed groups and political factions, opening the path for a new wave of violence.

In 2001, former President Kolingba tried to seize power, prompting Patassé to seek assistance from Jean-Pierre Bemba, leader of the Ugandan-backed rebel group, the Mouvement de Liberation du Congo (MLC).[5] The MLC had been active in neighbouring Democratic Republic of the Congo, occupying most of the northern part of the country bordering CAR. Ultimately, the coup failed. In the aftermath, Patassé accused his chief of staff Bozizé of disloyalty. Bozizé then fled to Chad but returned a year later to oust Patassé. Bozizé's troops quickly reached the capital of Bangui, resulting in heavy fighting. In order to contain the invading forces, Patassé again requested help from Jean-Pierre Bemba. Bemba's Banyamulenge troops pushed the rebel back to the north, but in the process committed mass atrocities against civilians. Ultimately, however, Bozizé was successful and seized power in 2003. Bozizé held power in a transitional government and was then elected president through general elections in 2005 in a contentious political process.

To this day, however, instability continues unabated, with various active rebel groups, mainly in the northern part of the country. Soon after the 2005 elections, violence broke out again in the northwest, causing the displacement of more than 100,000 civilians.[6] Among the armed groups involved, the Popular Army for the Restoration of the Republic and Democracy (APRD) was the most prominent, with members of Patassé's former presidential guard and local self-defense groups seeking security for their communities. Aside from the political power struggle, the rebellion in the northwest is fuelled by the situation of chronic insecurity, where civilians decided to take up arms against bandits known as *zaraguinas* who have preyed on the villages for years.[7] APRD's main targets have been government installations and its forces have been responsible for kidnapping, extortion, forced recruitment of children, and looting. CAR's presidential guard responded by carrying out a "dirty war" against the rebels, which has resulted in attacks on the civilian population, burning thousands of civilian homes, and summary executions.[8]

In 2006, violence in the northeast of the country broke out as a second rebellion was lead by another former associate of Patassé, Damane Zakaria, now chief of The Union of Democratic Forces for Unity (UFDR). The UFDR seized several towns, while the government of CAR accused Sudan of being behind these attacks.[9] The violence resulted in hundreds of civilian deaths and led to widespread burning of homes, looting, summary executions, and the use of child soldiers.[10]

---

5   Kolingba was president of CAR between 1981 and 1993. He seized power from Dacko through a coup and lost it to Patassé in the 1993 presidential elections.

6   Peter Bouckaert, Olivier Bercault and Human Rights Watch, *State of Anarchy: Rebellion and Abuses Against Civilians*. New York, NY: Human Rights Watch, 2007. UN OCHA *Central African Republic Fact Sheet*, June 2007.

7   Ibid.

8   Ibid.

9   *CAR Rebels Seize Town Near Chad*, BBC NEWS, sec. 2009, 30 October 2006 (accessed October 23, 2009).

10   Bouckaert, Bercault and Human Rights Watch, *State of Anarchy: Rebellion and Abuses Against Civilians*.

After years of continuous fighting, the country saw signs of progress toward ending the conflict in June 2008 when UFDR and APRD signed a peace agreement with the government to disarm and demobilize their soldiers.[11] Parliament approved amnesty legislation later that year, which covers violence from 15 March 2003.[12] Although the Amnesty Act does not cover international crimes as defined by the ICC, it does extend amnesty for serious crimes committed by Bozizé's army and presidential guard, the CAR rebel groups, and a more limited scope of potential crimes committed by Ange-Félix Patassé and several of his associates.[13] In December 2008, the CAR government and rival rebel groups ratified a resolution to create a Truth and Reconciliation Commission; however the mechanisms for its implementation are yet to be defined. More recently, the process culminated with the creation of a national unity government incorporating two rebel leaders in early 2009.[14]

INVOLVEMENT OF THE ICC

During 2002 and 2003, widespread violence committed by all parties, including Bemba's troops, prompted local human rights organizations affiliated with the International Federation for Human Rights to investigate serious crimes in the most affected neighbourhoods of the capital.[15] The evidence was sent to the newly established ICC to suggest investigation, and in December 2004 the government of CAR officially referred the situation to the Court. The Prosecutor opened an investigation in May 2007. In May of the following year the ICC Pre-Trial Chamber issued the first arrest warrant in the situation of CAR, against Jean-Pierre Bemba.[16] Bemba, travelling in Belgium at the time, was arrested the day after the warrant was unsealed and was subsequently transferred to The Hague. In 2009, the Pre-Trial Chamber confirmed charges of two crimes against humanity (rape and murder) and three war crimes (rape, murder, and pillage), as a military leader. To date, he is the only person facing trial in the situation of CAR. The trial is set to start in 2010.

The Study

OBJECTIVES

Since 2007, the Initiative for Vulnerable Populations at UC Berkeley's Human Rights Center has undertaken research to document the experience of conflict-affected populations and give voice to survi-

---

11   International Crisis Group, *Central African Republic: Untangling the Political Dialogue*, 2008.

12   Thijs Bouwknegt. *Central African Republic: amnesty for peace. Radio Netherlands Worldwide*, http://static.rnw.nl/migratie /www.rnw.nl/internationaljustice/icc/CAR/080930-car-amnesty-redirected (September 30, 2008).

13   International Center for Transitional Justice, *Regional Dynamics in Central Africa: Confronting Past Crimes at the National Level*, www.ictj.org/static/Factsheets/ICTJ_CAR_fs2009.pdf (accessed October 23, 2009).

14   *Touadera Names Rebels in New Central African Republic Govt, AFP*, sec. 2008, 9 December 2008 (accessed October 23, 2009).

15   Marlies Glasius, *We ourselves, we are part of the Functioning: The ICC, Victims, and Civil Society in the Central African Republic*, African Affairs, 108 (430) 2008: 49-67. International Federation for Human Rights. *War Crimes in the Central African Republic: 'When the Elephants Fight, the Grass Suffers'*. Paris: IFHR; 2003.

16   International Criminal Court, *Prosecutor opens investigation in the Central African Republic* (The Hague: ICC Press Release, 2007).

vors of mass violence. The survey in CAR aimed to capture opinions and attitudes about the impact of past and ongoing conflicts on the population and attitudes about peace, justice, and social reconstruction. The specific objectives of the survey were to:

- Assess the overall exposure to violence among the population as a result of war and human rights abuses, as well as incidents of domestic violence, since 2002

- Understand the priorities and needs of civilians affected by the armed conflict

- Measure the sense of security and levels of protection perceived by the population

- Examine social cohesion and community participation

- Capture attitudes about peace and social reconstruction, including the reintegration of former combatants

- Capture opinions and attitudes about different conflict-resolution and justice mechanisms, including perceptions of the national court system and the International Criminal Court

The methodology and objectives of the study are similar to other studies conducted by the Initiative in Cambodia, the Democratic Republic of Congo, and Uganda. However, the questionnaire and methodology reflect the specificity of the nature and concerns prevailing in CAR at the time of the survey. The research findings are aimed at supporting nongovernmental organizations, government and international agencies, and local and international courts in developing a strategic response to the violence and humanitarian crisis in CAR.

RESEARCH DESIGN AND SAMPLE

This report is based on a cross-sectional survey of adult residents in five administrative regions of the Central African Republic: the capital city Bangui, and the prefectures of Lobaye, Ombella M'Poko, Ouham, and Ouham Pende. The four prefectures and Bangui were selected to reflect the range of experience of conflicts in the CAR and to provide geographic representation from North to South. Together, they account for over half the population of CAR (52%).

Within each region, we used a systematic random selection method to sample villages proportionately to the population size, then households, and finally individuals, for interviews. Villages were randomly selected from a comprehensive list of villages for each selected prefecture using the 2003 general population census data.[17] A total of 117 villages were selected, and 6 villages had to be replaced by the nearest accessible village because of local instability or inaccessibility.

Within the villages, interviewers were assigned to zones where they selected every other household in a randomly chosen direction, starting from the center of the zone. In each household, defined as a group of people normally sleeping under the same roof and eating together, interviewers randomly selected one adult to be interviewed from a list of all eligible adults. Three attempts were made to contact a household or individual before replacing them with another.

---

17 3ème Recensement Général de la Population et de l'Habitation de 2003 (RGPH03).

The minimum sample size for each of the prefectures and Bangui was 352 individuals, for a total sample size of 1,760. Out of 2,192 households approached for interviews, 1,879 agreed to participate (86% participation rate). Within these 1,879 households, a total of 1,969 individuals were approached, and 1,879 participated in the interviews (95% participation rate, one individual selected per participating household).

The Committee for the Protection of Human Subjects at the University of California, Berkeley, reviewed and approved the study protocol in October 2009. In CAR, where no similar review board exists, the protocol was reviewed and approved by the Ministry of Economy, Planning, and International Cooperation. Approval to conduct interviews was also obtained from the local authorities at each survey site. Informed consent was sought for each selected participant; neither monetary nor material incentives were offered for participation.

RESEARCH INSTRUMENTS

Interviews were conducted using a standardized semi-structured questionnaire covering (1) respondents' demographics, (2) priorities and services, (3) health, (4) social cohesion and community relations, (5) security and conflict resolution, (6) domestic violence, (7) peace, (8) justice and accountability, (9) the International Criminal Court, (10) non-judicial measures for victims and reparations, (11) exposure to violence, and (12) psychological impact of the conflicts. The questionnaire was developed by experts in the field and after consultation with local experts. Response options based on pilot interviews were provided to the interviewer for coding but were never read to study participants with the exception of questions employing a scaling format (e.g., Likert scale). An open-ended field was always available to record complete responses.

The questionnaire and consent documents were first developed in French and then independently translated into Sango, the primary local language spoken throughout the country. An independent back-translation and pilot surveys were used to finalize and validate the instruments. Once the questionnaire was finalized, it was programmed into a Personal Digital Assistant (PDA)

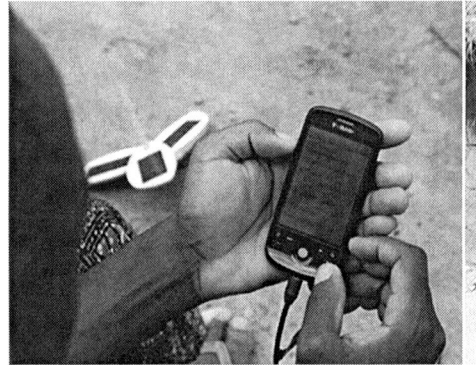

FIGURE I: DIGITAL DATA COLLECTION

using KoBo, our custom data collection package.[18] The use of PDAs allows enumerators to enter the data directly as they conduct interviews. The forms contain a built-in verification system that reduces the risk of skipping questions or entering erroneous values, resulting in higher quality of data. Daily synchronization with a central computer allows the lead researchers to check data for consistency and outliers during data collection.

---

18   Since 2007, the Human Rights Center has been developing tools to facilitate electronic data collection.

DATA COLLECTION AND ANALYSIS

Data collection took place during six weeks between November and December 2009. Five teams of two men and two women, for a total of twenty interviewers, implemented the study under the guidance of the lead researchers. The interviewers were university students or professionals with research experience. Prior to data collection, they participated in an eight-day training workshop that covered the study objectives and content, survey and interview techniques, use of the PDA, and trouble-shooting and solving technical problems.[19] The training included mock interviews and pilot-testing with randomly selected individuals at non-sampled sites.

At the survey sites, each interviewer was expected to conduct four interviews per day, each lasting an average of one hour. One-on-one interviews were conducted anonymously in a confidential setting. Due to the sensitivity of some of the questions, the interviewers were assigned to same-sex respondents. Upon selection of study participants, oral rather than written informed consent was obtained because of the high illiteracy rate in CAR. After data collection, the data were imported for analysis with the Statistical Package for Social Science (SPSS). All the results presented here accounted for the complex sampling methodology and weight factors.

LIMITATIONS

There are several limitations inherent to the method and context of the study. The sample was designed to be representative of the region under study, not for the whole of CAR, since only part of the country was included in the survey. Some villages, households, and individuals had to be replaced, and it is unknown how the individuals replaced might differ from those interviewed. In addition, it is possible that responses were influenced by inaccurate recall, social desirability, and concerns over safety in areas affected by armed conflict. The training, use of a consent form, anonymous interviews, confidentiality, supervision, and quality control were all designed to reduce biases and errors. Constructs and terminology used for this study were not defined or explained to the participants to avoid influencing them. As a result, they were free to interpret those concepts based on their own understanding. To address this limitation, we asked respondents to define key concepts (e.g., peace, justice), and throughout the questionnaire, we carefully chose phrasing and translation that would avoid misunderstanding.

---

19   The PDAs are designed to be used by surveyors with no or little computer experience.

RESPONDENT CHARACTERISTICS

THE SURVEY WAS CONDUCTED in the capital city, Bangui, and four out of sixteen prefectures: Lobaye, Ombella M'Poko, Ouham and Ouham Pende. The prefectures were selected to reflect the range of experience of armed conflict in CAR and to provide a geographic unity from North to South. Other areas affected by conflict were not included in this study but should be considered for future research. A total of 1,879 interviews were conducted in 117 villages and neighborhoods. The results are representative for the population at the prefecture level.

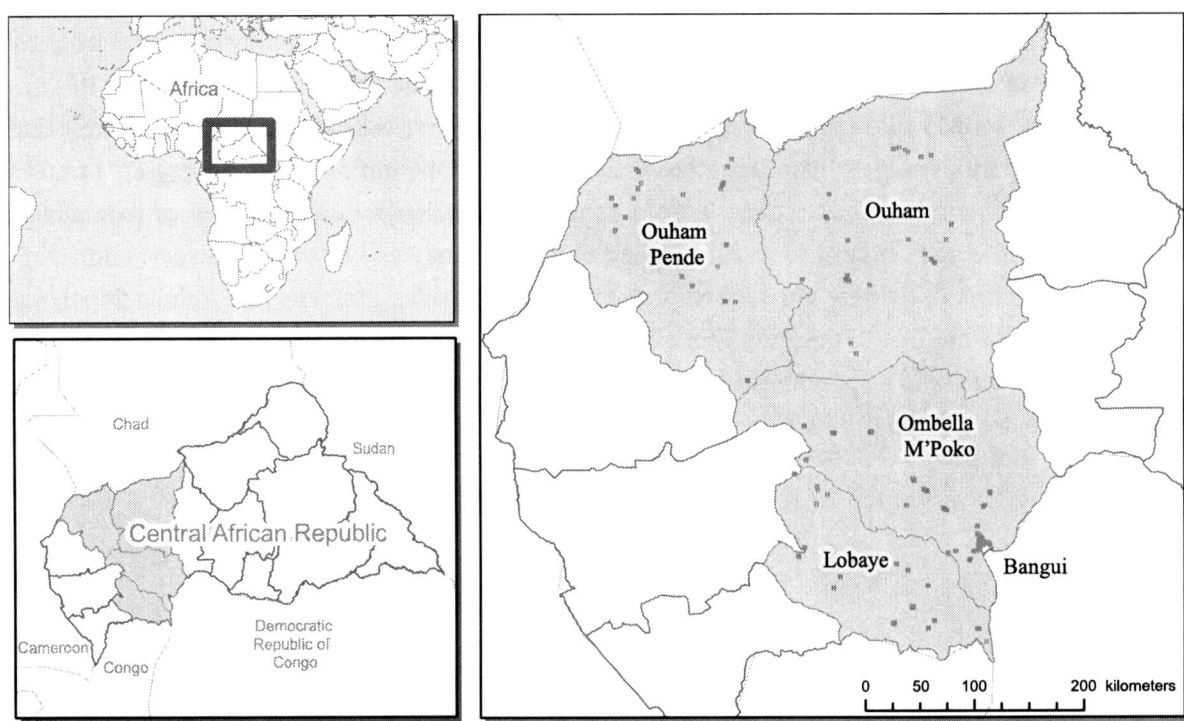

FIGURE 2: SAMPLE DISTRIBUTION

The interview teams were composed of equal numbers of men and women and were assigned to same-sex respondents. The mean age of respondents was 36 years. The ethnic composition of the sample is broad, with the largest groups being the Gbaya (24%), Karre (14%), Banda (11%), and Manza

(9%). The ethnic composition varied greatly across prefectures, as illustrated in the following figure. The majority of respondents described themselves as married or in a partnership (75%), 12 percent reported being single and never having been married, while 8 percent were widowed and 6 percent were divorced.

The average level of education was low, with 25 percent of respondents reporting no formal education, and 29 percent reporting incomplete primary education. The literacy level found in this survey (50%) is consistent with nationwide alphabetization rate estimate (44% in 2008), and below the regional average for sub-Saharan Africa (62% for the 2000-2007 period).[20] Educational achievements were lowest in the northern prefectures of Ouham and Ouham Pende, where over 75 percent reported no or incomplete primary education. Those two prefectures also claimed the highest proportion of asset-poor households.[21] The data suggested that more than 30 percent of the respondents were asset poor in Ouham and Ouham Pende, compared to 10 percent or less in Bangui, Lobaye, and Ombella M'Poko.

		Bangui	Lobaye	Ombella M'Poko	Ouham	Ouham Pende	Total
	Sex (% women)	50%	50%	50%	50%	50%	50%
	Age	36.7	36.3	36.0	35.9	36.7	36.4
Matrimonial Status	Married, partner	64%	79%	75%	81%	82%	75%
	Single, never married	20%	10%	11%	6%	6%	12%
	Widow(er)	8%	7%	7%	10%	8%	8%
	Divorced	8%	4%	7%	4%	4%	6%
Education level	None	6%	23%	19%	48%	41%	25%
	Incomplete primary	19%	36%	31%	30%	36%	29%
	Complete primary	14%	18%	14%	10%	7%	12%
	Secondary incomplete	39%	19%	28%	10%	15%	24%
	Secondary complete	10%	2%	5%	0%	1%	5%
	Technical/Professional school	2%	1%	1%	1%	1%	1%
	University or higher	10%	1%	2%	0%	0%	4%
	Other	0%	0%	0%	0%	0%	0%
Literacy	% read yes	79%	44%	51%	23%	33%	50%
Assets	% poorest quintile	1%	10%	6%	39%	33%	17%

---

20   Enquête Centrafricaine pour le Suivi Evaluation du Bien être (ECASEB), Institut Centrafricain des Statistiques et des Etudes Economiques et Sociales, 2008; State of the World's Children, UNICEF, 2009.

21   Asset poverty is a common measure of poverty based on ownership of a set of common household items. In this study, we assessed ownership of 9 items. Respondents could have a score ranging from 0 (no items owned) to 9 (all items owned). Asset poor are defined as the respondents among the lowest quintile of asset ownership. While it is not a measure of absolute poverty, the indicator suggests the geographic distribution of poverty. It does not, however, allow for cross-country comparisons because the set of assets may vary.

Ethnicity							
	Gbaya	22%	30%	16%	42%	16%	24%
	Karre	2%	1%	1%	0%	60%	14%
	Banda	20%	4%	7%	15%	1%	11%
	Manza (Mandja, Mandjia)	18%	2%	15%	5%	1%	9%
	Gbanou	3%	2%	27%	2%	1%	6%
	Yakoma	15%	2%	3%	0%	0%	5%
	Kaba	3%	1%	3%	6%	11%	5%
	Dagba	1%	0%	1%	24%	0%	5%
	Ngbaka-Bantou	3%	20%	6%	0%	0%	4%
	Mbati	2%	14%	4%	0%	0%	3%
	Mboum	1%	0%	0%	0%	7%	2%
	Ali	0%	4%	7%	1%	0%	2%
	Bati	1%	11%	1%	1%	0%	2%
	Other	0%	0%	0%	0%	0%	0%

BUILDING A LASTING PEACE ANYWHERE requires the establishment of security, a legitimate government, institutional reforms to protect civil liberties and the rule of law, revitalization of the economy and civil society, and the promotion of social reconstruction and reconciliation.[22] In this section, we discuss individuals' exposure to violence and their perception of various processes that contribute to building a sustainable peace.

Priorities: Peace First

To better understand respondents' opinions of the way to move toward peace, we first asked them to define their current top priority. Reflecting the ongoing political instability and conflict, peace is the most frequently mentioned priority (32%). When asked about the meaning of peace, respondents define it as a broad social concept that goes beyond the absence of violence and includes the absence of fear (47%), living together united (39%), freedom (34%), having basic needs fulfilled (29%), the absence of violence (26%), a good economy (21%), and health and education services (15%).

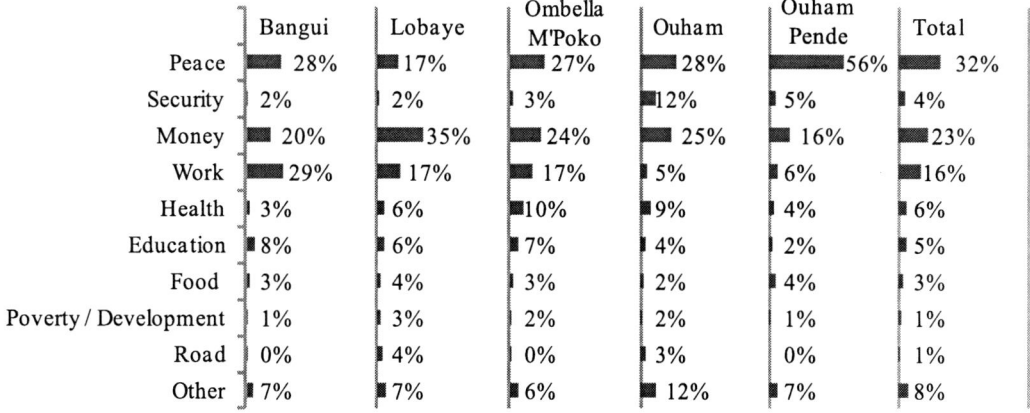

	Bangui	Lobaye	Ombella M'Poko	Ouham	Ouham Pende	Total
Peace	28%	17%	27%	28%	56%	32%
Security	2%	2%	3%	12%	5%	4%
Money	20%	35%	24%	25%	16%	23%
Work	29%	17%	17%	5%	6%	16%
Health	3%	6%	10%	9%	4%	6%
Education	8%	6%	7%	4%	2%	5%
Food	3%	4%	3%	2%	4%	3%
Poverty / Development	1%	3%	2%	2%	1%	1%
Road	0%	4%	0%	3%	0%	1%
Other	7%	7%	6%	12%	7%	8%

FIGURE 3: RESPONDENTS' TOP PRIORITIES

22   Nicole Ball, "The Challenge of Rebuilding War-Torn Societies," in *Turbulent Peace: The Challenges of Managing International Conflicts*, ed. Chester A. Crocker, Fen Osler Hampson and Pamela R. Aall (Washington, DC: United States Institute of Peace Press, 2001).

Livelihood concerns are also frequently mentioned among respondents' top priorities, including money (23%), work (16%), and services including health (6%) and education (5%). These priorities reflect respondents' current living conditions and lack of access to social services. Many of the villages sampled in the survey lacked infrastructure or supplies and had no official teachers. When asked to rank a range of services, few respondents found them good or very good. Only one-third of them ranked their access to water as good or very good. One in four or less ranked their access to education and health services as good or very good. Indeed, while such services are generally available in urban center and large villages, they are often lacking or of poor quality in rural areas.

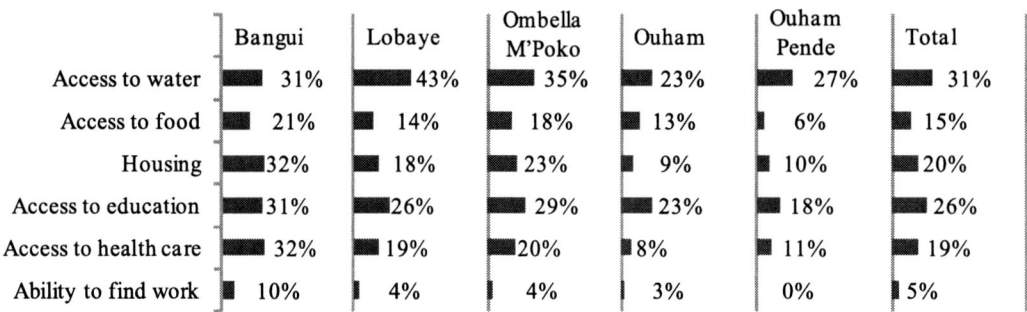

	Bangui	Lobaye	Ombella M'Poko	Ouham	Ouham Pende	Total
Access to water	31%	43%	35%	23%	27%	31%
Access to food	21%	14%	18%	13%	6%	15%
Housing	32%	18%	23%	9%	10%	20%
Access to education	31%	26%	29%	23%	18%	26%
Access to health care	32%	19%	20%	8%	11%	19%
Ability to find work	10%	4%	4%	3%	0%	5%

FIGURE 4: RANKING OF SERVICES (% GOOD – VERY GOOD)

Security and Exposure to Violence

SECURITY

Many respondents included "absence of violence" (26%) and "freedom from fear" (47%) in their definition of peace. This finding suggests that increasing security and restoring a sense of safety must be part of any peace-building effort. Respondents continue to report insecurity and a lack a safety or protection. They were asked to rank their perceived physical safety in a range of daily situations, from "very good" to "very bad." The highest percentages of respondents reporting "bad" or "very bad" safety in the proposed situations were found in Ouham and Ouham Pende. In Ouham Pende, up to 46 percent reported a bad or very bad sense of safety walking at night in their village. High percentages of bad or very bad reported safety in the proposed situations were also found in the capital city, Bangui. The situations in which respondents most frequently reported a "poor" or "very poor" sense of safety include walking at night in the city/village, meeting strangers, and going to the nearest village or town.

When asked who provides them with security, 54 percent of respondents reported "God." Respondents were allowed more than one answer, and 15 percent mentioned themselves. Half of the respondents (46%) only mentioned God, themselves, or nobody as providing security. Clearly the security sector has failed to provide protection. Less than half (45%) mentioned government forces including the government itself (21%), the Presidential/Republican Guard (Guarde Presidentielle / Republicaines [GP/GR], 13%), the Central African Armed Forces (Forces Armées Centrafricaines [FACA], 15%), and the Police/Gendarmes (3%).

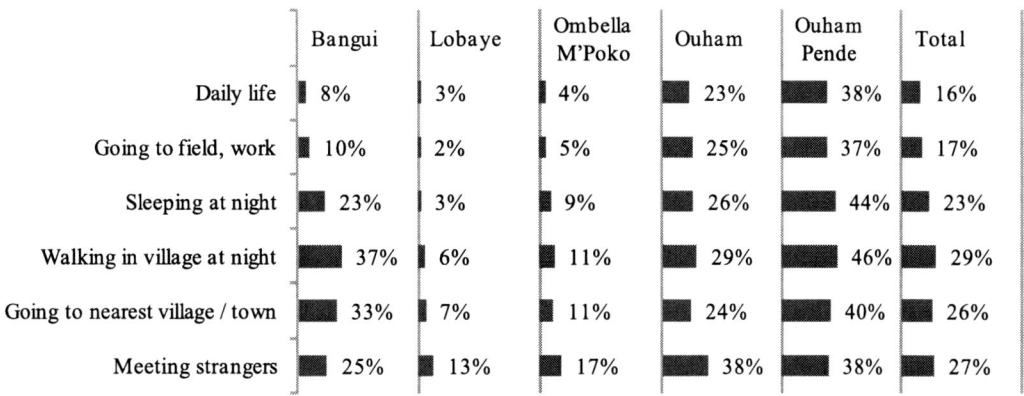

	Bangui	Lobaye	Ombella M'Poko	Ouham	Ouham Pende	Total
Daily life	8%	3%	4%	23%	38%	16%
Going to field, work	10%	2%	5%	25%	37%	17%
Sleeping at night	23%	3%	9%	26%	44%	23%
Walking in village at night	37%	6%	11%	29%	46%	29%
Going to nearest village / town	33%	7%	11%	24%	40%	26%
Meeting strangers	25%	13%	17%	38%	38%	27%

FIGURE 5: SELF REPORTED POOR OR VERY POOR SENSE OF SAFETY (%)

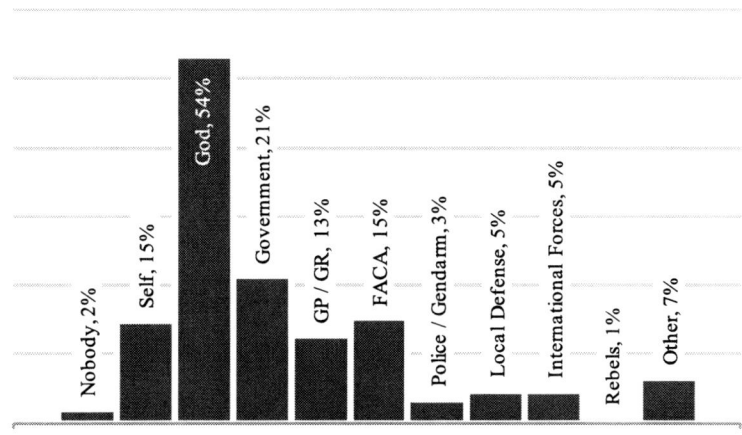

FIGURE 6: PROTECTION

EXPOSURE TO VIOLENCE

Respondents' perceived lack of security is reinforced by their frequent exposure to violent events. The following figure illustrates respondents' exposure to a list of 24 traumatic events. Among respondents, 76 percent reported witnessing at least one violent event committed by armed groups: 64 percent had witnessed pillaging, 59 percent had witnessed combat, 54 percent had witnessed beatings, 35 percent had witnessed killing, and 21 percent had witnessed sexual violence.

A large number of respondents reported direct experience related to the conflict, including displacement (79%) and forced separation from household members (56%). Fewer had direct experience of violence, including being physically attacked, beaten, or tortured (20%), being held prisoner by armed groups (11%), or being abducted (10%). Respondents also reported coercion by armed groups: 14 percent reported they were forced to work, 5 percent reported they were forced to participate in pillaging, and 2 percent reported they had been forced to beat someone. All the events were more frequently reported in the northern prefectures of Ouham and Ouham Pende.

	Bangui	Lobaye	Ombella M'Poko	Ouham	Ouham Pende	Total	Last 12 months
Witness combat	66%	23%	53%	64%	72%	59%	6%
Witness pillage	61%	30%	51%	81%	84%	64%	12%
Witness beating	50%	23%	41%	65%	80%	54%	12%
Witness killing	31%	13%	27%	47%	51%	35%	6%
Witness sexual abuse	16%	10%	13%	27%	38%	21%	4%
Goods, property stolen, destroyed	50%	22%	46%	85%	89%	61%	8%
Flee home / village	73%	42%	73%	96%	96%	79%	9%
Currently displaced	8%	7%	10%	9%	13%	9%	
Separate from household members	52%	25%	51%	65%	76%	56%	6%
Physically attacked, beaten, tortured	14%	4%	13%	23%	42%	20%	4%
Being in the middle of fighting	25%	7%	21%	33%	46%	28%	3%
Threatened with death	30%	12%	26%	43%	57%	35%	6%
Think will die	55%	33%	55%	91%	84%	65%	8%
Household members killed	31%	17%	27%	48%	57%	37%	4%
Prisoner	4%	1%	4%	17%	28%	11%	2%
Abducted	5%	1%	4%	13%	27%	10%	2%
Abducted for at least a week	1%	0%	1%	4%	18%	5%	1%
Forced to work	6%	2%	7%	25%	29%	14%	4%
Forced to pillage	2%	0%	2%	8%	14%	5%	2%
Forced to beat someone	1%	0%	1%	3%	6%	2%	1%
Forced to kill	1%	0%	0%	1%	2%	1%	0%
Sexually abused by armed groups	3%	1%	3%	2%	8%	4%	1%
Sexually abused other than armed groups	3%	2%	3%	4%	6%	4%	1%
Forced to sexually abuse	1%	1%	1%	1%	4%	2%	0%
Sexually abused by armed groups (women)	5%	1%	6%	3%	14%	6%	1%
Sexually abused other than armed groups (women)	3%	4%	6%	8%	11%	6%	2%

FIGURE 7: EXPOSURE TO VIOLENCE

Among all respondents, 4 percent reported having experienced sexual violations committed by armed groups, and the same percentage (4%) reported sexual violence by individuals other than armed groups. Reports of sexual violence by armed groups was significantly higher among women (6%) compared to men (1%). Sexual violence was especially prevalent in Ouham Pende, where 14 percent of the women reported having experienced it. Beyond the physical and direct violence, two-thirds of respondents (65%) reported thinking they would die at some point during the conflict.

Incidence data further show the ongoing nature of the violence, especially in the prefectures of Ouham and Ouham Pende. In those prefectures, over 10 percent of the respondents reported having witnessed pillaging and beating, having been forced to flee their home or village, having property stolen or destroyed, and being threatened with death over the last 12 months. These data show that civilians in CAR, as in other places affected by mass violence, have paid a high toll during the successive conflicts. This survey documents for the first time the extent of the violence.

DOMESTIC VIOLENCE

In addition to exposure to conflict-related violence, the survey asked respondents about their experience of domestic violence. Fourteen percent of respondents reported they had already been seriously physically beaten by someone from their household. However, the results show great gender disparity: 22 percent of the women reported serious physical beating by a household member compared to 4 percent of the men.

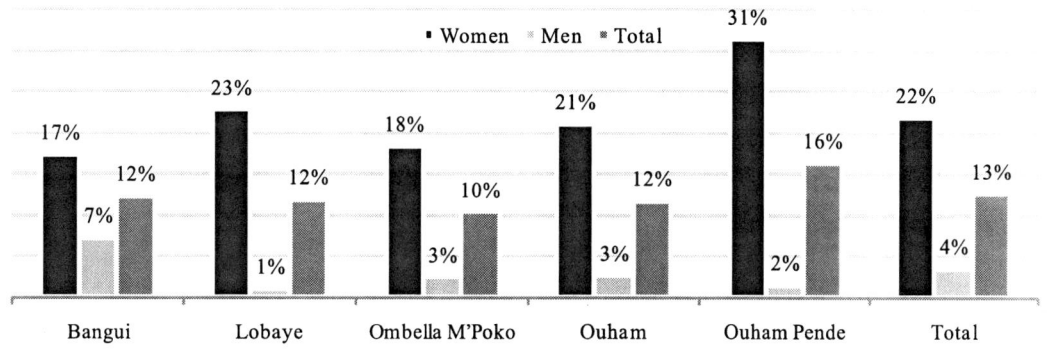

FIGURE 8: DOMESTIC VIOLENCE

Among women, the main reason reported for the beatings were disobeying (42%), arguing (30%), jealousy (12%), serving dinner late (8%), and alcohol (8%).

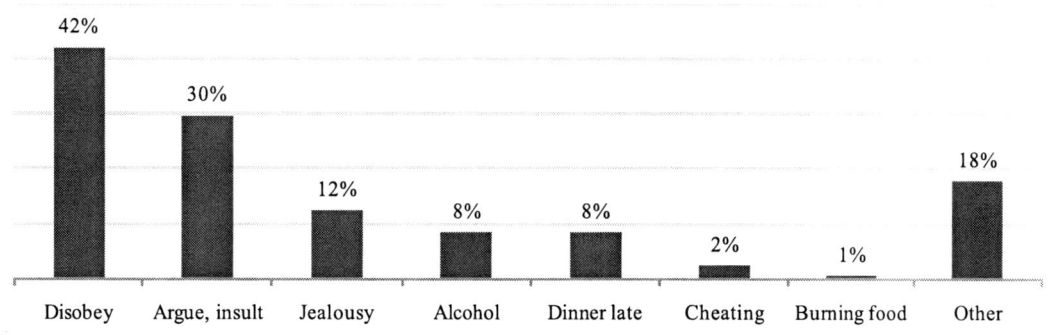

FIGURE 9: REASONS FOR DOMESTIC VIOLENCE

Respondents were further asked under what circumstances a serious physical beating of a household member would be acceptable. Over half respondents (58%) found no circumstances would justify such beating. One-third of respondents said it would be acceptable to beat a household member who disobeyed (33%) or those who argue or insult (17%). Only a minority said a beating would be acceptable for cheating (4%), serving dinner late (1%), or burning the food (<1%). As many as 39 percent of respondents said they themselves had severely beaten a household member in such conditions. It is important to note that this includes spousal abuse and the beating of children. This may explain why 44 percent of the women had been involved in seriously beating a household member.

Achieving Peace

ORIGINS OF THE CONFLICTS

As discussed above, peace is the most frequently cited priority among study respondents. In order to understand the population's perception of what needs to be done to achieve peace, we first need to understand what, in their opinion, are the root causes of the conflict. For a majority (61%), the root cause is fighting over power among the political elites. About a third (33%) believed the conflict to be rooted in poverty, and 22 percent mentioned ethnic divisions. Respondents were allowed to provide several answers and a range of other causes, often interlinked, including exploitation of natural resources, money, and access to land were identified. The respondents' perceived root causes of the conflicts are consistent with the literature that accuses "the militarization of [CAR] politics and the ethnic exclusiveness of successive governments."[23] At the same time structural problems, including deep poverty, are also identified as root causes of violence.

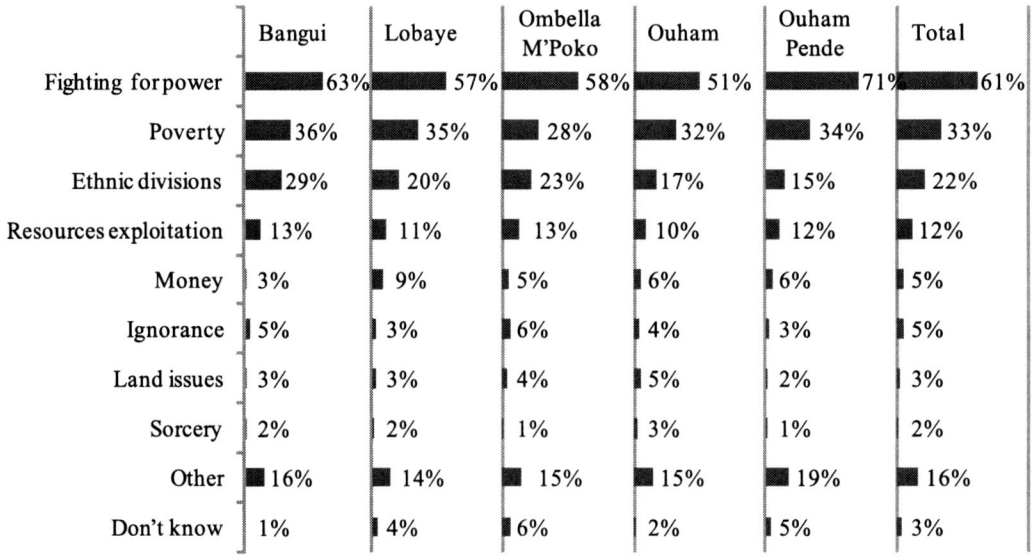

	Bangui	Lobaye	Ombella M'Poko	Ouham	Ouham Pende	Total
Fighting for power	63%	57%	58%	51%	71%	61%
Poverty	36%	35%	28%	32%	34%	33%
Ethnic divisions	29%	20%	23%	17%	15%	22%
Resources exploitation	13%	11%	13%	10%	12%	12%
Money	3%	9%	5%	6%	6%	5%
Ignorance	5%	3%	6%	4%	3%	5%
Land issues	3%	3%	4%	5%	2%	3%
Sorcery	2%	2%	1%	3%	1%	2%
Other	16%	14%	15%	15%	19%	16%
Don't know	1%	4%	6%	2%	5%	3%

FIGURE 10: PERCEIVED ROOT CAUSES OF THE CONFLICTS

23   International Crisis Group. *Africa Report N°136: Central African Republic: Anatomy of a Phantom State.* Nairobi/Brussels: ICG; 2007.

MEANS FOR PEACE

Next, we asked respondents if they believed it is possible for the people in CAR to live together peace-fully or to live peacefully with neighboring countries. For both questions, about one half of the population responded affirmatively, but nearly one in four respondents did not believe it was possible. The rest were uncertain. Perhaps because of the chronic security and economic problems in the north, respondents in Ouham and Ouham Pende generally felt least confident that peace is possible.

Is it possible for people in CAR to live together peacefully? (% total)   Is it possible to live peacefully with neighboring countries? (% total)

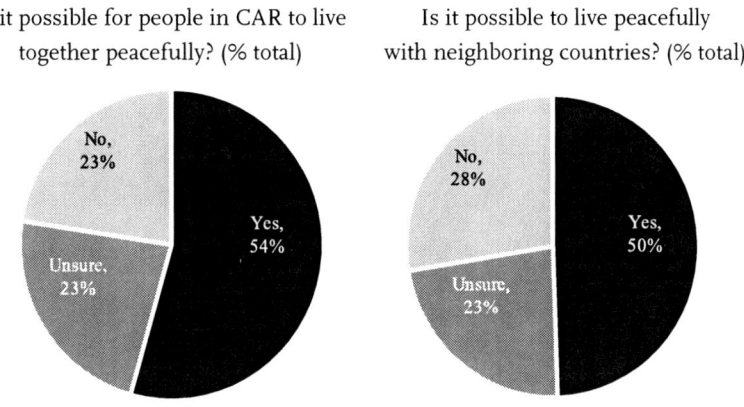

FIGURE II: ACHEIVING PEACE

When asked what needs to be done to achieve lasting peace in CAR, over half of respondents mentioned political dialogue was needed, 23 percent mentioned elections, 17 percent mentioned that armed groups need to be disarmed, 16 percent said there needs to be some sort of reconciliation or rebuilding of unity, and 9 percent said political power should be shared. Few supported a military solution.

	Bangui	Lobaye	Ombella M'Poko	Ouham	Ouham Pende	Total
Dialog	70%	51%	54%	42%	50%	56%
Have elections	14%	26%	20%	22%	38%	23%
Disarm groups	18%	17%	14%	18%	17%	17%
Reconcile, unite	14%	18%	20%	8%	21%	16%
Share political power	14%	10%	10%	6%	3%	9%
Reform the military	6%	7%	7%	6%	5%	6%
Pray	5%	4%	5%	6%	8%	6%
Defeat armed groups	2%	2%	4%	15%	5%	5%
Change government	7%	7%	4%	7%	2%	6%
Chase away bad spirits	5%	4%	5%	6%	4%	5%
Provide work	4%	6%	4%	3%	2%	4%
Other	13%	11%	12%	11%	14%	12%

FIGURE 12: MEANS TO ACHIEVE PEACE

ELECTIONS AND PARTICIPATION IN SOCIETY

Holding free and fair elections and respecting civil and political rights have been core elements of contemporary peace-building practices. However, elections can also drive parties apart rather than reconcile them.[24] Considering CAR's history of coups, counter-coups and recurrent violence, elections present a risky situation. Presidential and parliamentary elections are scheduled in CAR in 2010. Struggles for political power have been a root cause of the violence here, yet many respondents see elections and changes in government as a step toward building peace.

A large majority of respondents (94%) plan to vote in the upcoming elections. Those who plan to vote say they will do so because it is their duty (38%), because they have to elect someone who will help the country (34%), or because elections will help bring peace and security (12%). Those who did not plan to vote claim they simply did not want to (28%), that it was useless (33%), and/or that they are not interested in politics (15%). Intentions to vote are consistent with actual voting behavior during the 2005 presidential elections. A majority of respondents (80%) said they voted in 2005 and those who did not were most frequently too young to have voted (39%). Most voters also felt confident they would be free to choose whom to vote for: 77 percent said they would be totally free, and 15 percent said they would be somewhat free to do so. Only 8 percent said they would not be free at all, or not very free to choose whom to vote for.

The survey also explored respondents' involvement in their community and society as a whole. Strengthening social ties within communities and between individuals and the state is critical to the transition from war to peace.[25] Overall, 85 percent of respondents reported being part of a group or association. The majority of them were members of a church or religious group (84%). The second most frequent type of group or association was farmers' associations, with 17 percent of the respondents reporting being part of such a group. Farmers' associations were especially frequent in Ouham Pende (42%). Other groups included youth groups (9%), women's associations (9%), political organizations (8%), and loan/credit groups (5%). Most respondents felt totally free (70%) or somewhat free (20%) to join any organization, while 10 percent felt not very free (6%) or not free at all (4%) to do so. However, respondents experienced freedom of expression less frequently. Only 43 percent felt totally free to say what they want. Freedom of expression was least frequently reported in Bangui, Ouham, and Ouham Pende, possibly because of the ongoing conflict and presence of armed groups.

While respondents reported active engagement in society, only one in four (28%) reported having contacted a leader of any sort (local, political, civil society, etc). In over half the cases (58%), respondents contacted a religious leader, while 24 percent contacted the local village chief, 14 percent contacted regional leaders such as a mayor, prefect, or deputy, and 14 percent contacted other government officials (12%). The subject matter of the contacts between individuals and leaders was not explored.

24 Paris R. "Peacebuilding and the Limits of Liberal Internationalism," *International Security*, Vol. 22, No. 2 (Autumn, 1997), 54-89; Paris R. "International peacebuilding and the 'mission civilisatrice'," *Review of International Studies* (2002), 28, 637–56.

25 Colletta, J. J. & Cullen, M. L. *Violent Conflict and the Transformation of Social Capital.* Washington, DC: International Bank for Reconstruction and Development/World Bank, 2000.

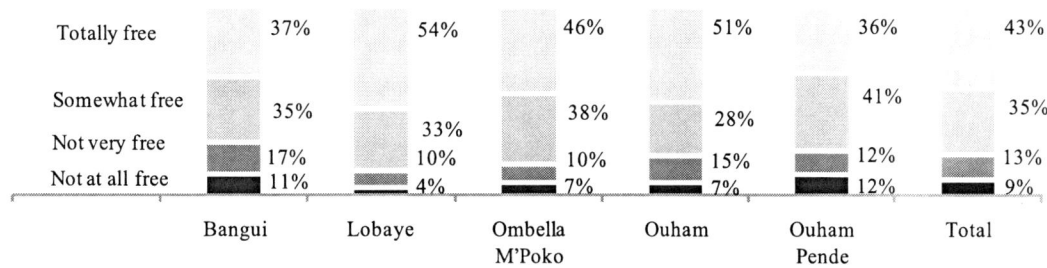

	Bangui	Lobaye	Ombella M'Poko	Ouham	Ouham Pende	Total
Totally free	37%	54%	46%	51%	36%	43%
Somewhat free	35%	33%	38%	28%	41%	35%
Not very free	17%	10%	10%	15%	12%	13%
Not at all free	11%	4%	7%	7%	12%	9%

FIGURE 13: SELF-REPORTED FREEDOM OF EXPRESSION

LOCAL CONFLICTS AND CONFLICT RESOLUTION

While the exposure to violence and peace-building questions were related to the large-scale conflict in CAR, this study also explored respondents' experience of local conflicts. One in four (25%) respondents mentioned having experienced some sort of conflict over the one-year period prior to the survey. Most of those reporting conflicts said the nature of the local disputes were domestic (48%) or concerned relations with neighbors (13%). Fewer than 10 percent reported conflict over theft (9%), building (7%), money lending/borrowing (6%), and land (5%). The conflicts were most frequently resolved within the family (40%), followed by the village chief (29%) or by religious leaders (15%). Police (5%) and the judicial system (4%) were rarely mentioned. Furthermore, the data on local conflicts and conflict resolution showed little variation across prefectures.

DDR AND PERCEPTION OF FORMER COMBATANTS

Former belligerents must be disarmed before progress toward peace can be made.[26] Yet, the demobilization, disarmament, and reintegration (DDR) of former combatants has been a challenging process. At the time of the survey, a DDR process had been initiated as a way to end the rebellions in the north, however, it has experienced several delays, causing tension between armed groups and the government. Still, some respondents held high expectations that the DDR process will contribute to peace: 17 percent mention disarmament as part of the means to achieve peace. The survey further asked respondents to rank their level of comfort in the presence of former combatants, regardless of the armed group they were affiliated with, in a range of hypothetical situations that reflect common daily events.

Overall, respondents were least comfortable sharing a drink with former combatants: 83 percent said they would be uncomfortable in that situation. In-depth interviews showed this was due first to the social function of sharing a drink, seen as a sign of cooperation and cohesion, and second to the fear that former combatants would become violent under the influence of alcohol. Respondents also frequently felt uncomfortable living in the same household (75%) or living as close neighbors (72%). Over half the respondents also felt uncomfortable having former combatants marry a household member (61%), working with former combatants (59%), sharing a meal (57%), and going to the same market

---

26   Chester A. Crocker and Fen Osler Hampson, "Making Peace Settlements Work," *Foreign Policy*, No. 104 (Autumn, 1996), 54–71.

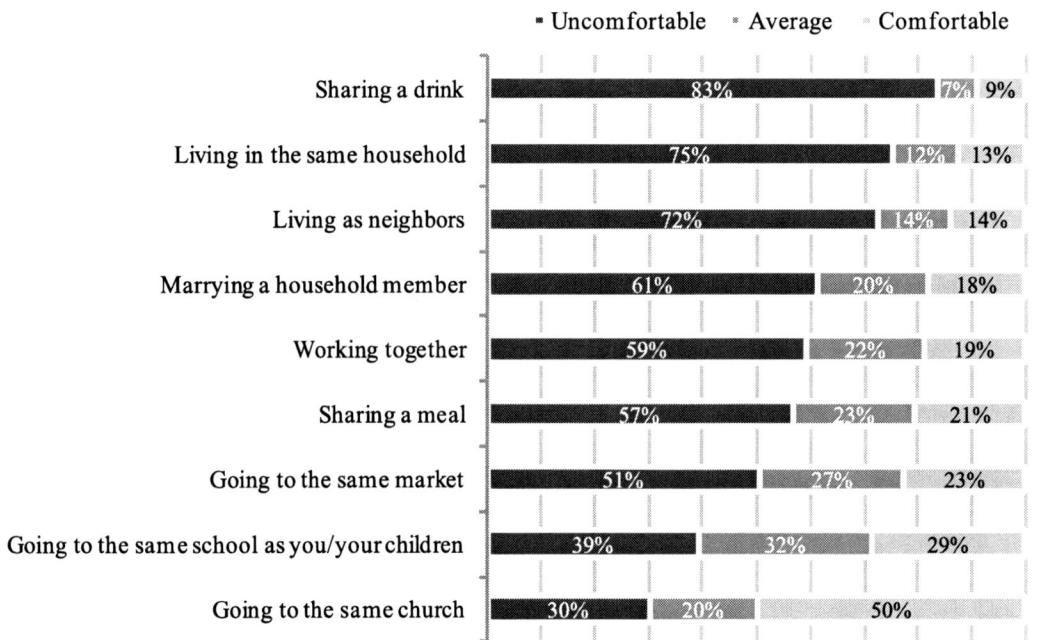

Sharing a drink	83%	7%	9%
Living in the same household	75%	12%	13%
Living as neighbors	72%	14%	14%
Marrying a household member	61%	20%	18%
Working together	59%	22%	19%
Sharing a meal	57%	23%	21%
Going to the same market	51%	27%	23%
Going to the same school as you/your children	39%	32%	29%
Going to the same church	30%	20%	50%

FIGURE 14: RESPONDENTS' PERCEIVED LEVEL OF
COMFORT TOWARDS FORMER COMBATANTS

(51%). The least stigmatizing situations were those where direct contact may not be necessary as when former combatants go to the same school (39%) or the same church (30%) as the respondents or their children. There were no or few differences across prefectures.

The results further suggest that while some respondents have high expectations for DDR, reintegration of former combatants in the community will not be easy. Interventions are needed to address the overall level of comfort interacting with former combatants in various settings and ensure that bridges are built between the community and former combatants. One possible strategy of the DDR program is to build education or outreach programs. A second strategy is to develop a community-based program that would provide the population opportunity to interact with former combatant in a non-threatening scenario. A third possible strategy is to develop an economic program that would include both former combatants and community members, permitting both to benefit from the DDR programs without the perception of favoring former combatants.

Information

Media is increasingly recognized for its potential role in peacebuilding and social marketing.[27] The study included several questions on access to media, consumption habits, and perception of the various sources of information. A quarter of respondents (24%) felt they were not at all informed about

27 Spurk, C. "Media and peacebuilding: Concepts, actors and challenges," SwissPeace Working Paper Series; 2002.

events and news about CAR, while about half (48%) said they were moderately informed, and 28 percent said they were very informed. They generally felt more informed about what happened at the local level, with 44 percent saying they were very informed, 43 percent moderately informed, and 13 percent not informed.

Main Source	Bangui	Lobaye	Ombella M'Poko	Ouham	Ouham Pende
Radio	72%	50%	61%	26%	33%
Friends, neighbors	19%	39%	32%	60%	53%
Local leaders	0%	8%	5%	5%	6%
Religious leaders	1%	2%	2%	2%	5%
Television	5%	0%	0%	0%	0%
Print media	2%	0%	0%	0%	1%
Other	1%	1%	0%	7%	2%

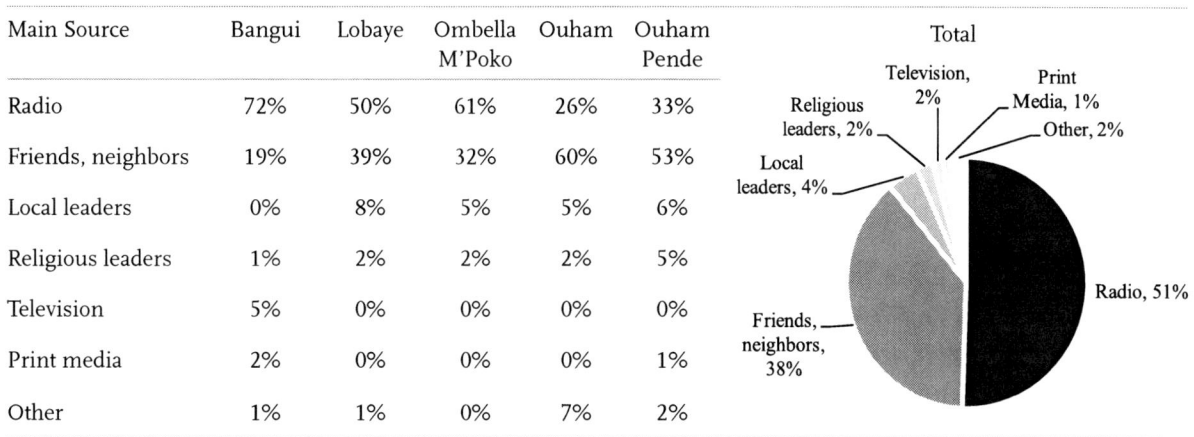

FIGURE 15: MAIN SOURCE OF INFORMATION

The primary sources of information were the radio (51%) or friends and neighbors (38%). Fewer respondents identified local (4%), or religious leaders (2%), the television (2%), print media (1%) or other sources as their primary sources of information. However, radio was less frequently the primary source of information in the northern prefectures of Ouham and Ouham Pende, a reflection of the prevailing poverty, with fewer households owning or having access to a radio.

When asked specifically about access to the radio, 41 percent of respondents said they never listened to a radio, and 59 percent indicated listening to a radio at least occasionally (36% on a daily basis). Respondents listened most frequently to the radio in the morning (5:00 to 10:00, 76%), and late afternoon (16:00 to 18:00, 52%). Compared to other prefectures, fewer respondents reported listening to a radio in the northern prefectures of Ouham and Ouham Pende (35% in both prefectures), and among those who did, few listened to a radio on a daily basis (approx. 40%).

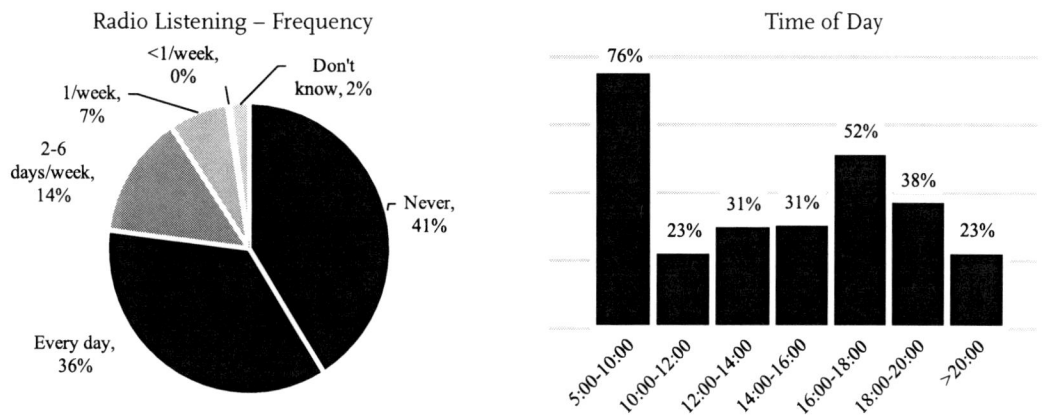

FIGURE 16: RADIO LISTENING HABITS

The most popular radio stations are Radio Centrafrique and Radio Ndeke Luka (respectively 66% and 62% of the respondents who listen to radio report listening to those radio stations). A quarter of the respondents listened to Radio Nehemie (24%) and RFI (23%). Over 10 percent of the respondents identify Afrique #1 (20%), and Radio ICDI (13%) as their radio of choice. Other radio stations were mentioned, some with regional importance. Radio Maria, for example, was favored by only 4 percent of the respondents overall, but was the preferred station in Ouham prefecture (34%).

The main type of radio programs people listened to is news broadcasts: 88 percent of those listening to a radio reported listening to the news. Other frequently mentioned programs include religious programs (36%); programs on democracy, peace, and justice (36%); announcements (35%); and programs on health (35%), and music or entertainment (31%).

As outlined above, newspapers and print media were seldom identified as the primary source of information. Nevertheless, 20 percent of those interviewed reported reading a newspaper at least occasionally: 3 percent read it on a daily basis, 7 percent read it more than once a week, 5 percent read it once a week, and 5 percent read it less than once a week. Reading newspapers was especially frequent in Bangui (45%) and to a lesser extent in Ombella M'Poko (18%) and Lobaye (11%). In Ouham and Ouham Pende, less than 10 percent of respondents reported reading a newspaper at least occasionally. This is likely due both to the low availability of newspapers and high level of illiteracy. Among those who read a newspaper, in Bangui, the most frequently read newspapers were *Le Citoyen* (60%), *Le Confident* (36%), and *L'Hirondelle* (22%). *Le Citoyen* was also read by over 50 percent of those reading newspapers in Ombella M'Poko and Lobaye. In Ouham and Ouham Pende, respondents reported reading mainly religious pamphlets and publications.

Overall, only 2 percent of the respondents identified television as their main source of information. However, 26 percent reported watching television at least occasionally, which is more than the number of respondents reading newspapers at least occasionally. Again, regional differences were important with 58 percent of those living in Bangui reporting watching television occasionally compared to 22 percent in Ombella M'Poko, 17 percent in Lobaye, 7 percent in Ouham Pende, and 3 percent in Ouham.

Finally, respondents were asked to rank their level of trust in the media on a scale from no trust at all to extremely trustful. The question was only asked to those using the media. Among those listening to the radio, 43 percent trusted it a lot or extremely. Among newspaper readers, fewer trusted it a lot or extremely (29%).

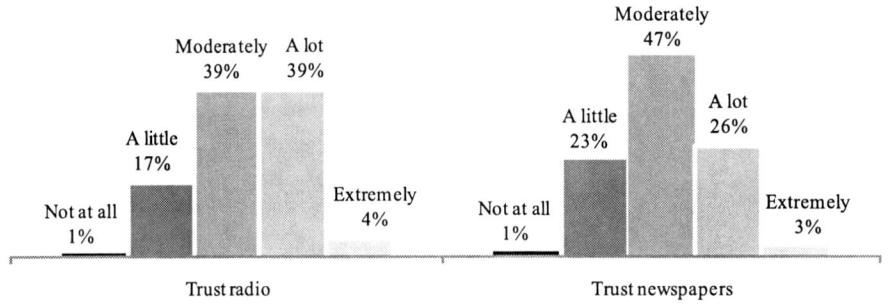

FIGURE 17: TRUST IN MEDIA

Accountability, Justice, and Forgiveness

ACCOUNTABILITY AND ATTITUDES TOWARD ALLEGED PERPETRATORS

Although accountability and justice were infrequently mentioned as top priorities (1%), nearly all respondents (98%) still believe it is important to hold accountable those responsible for the violence committed during the conflicts. This is consistent with what we have found in other studies. For example, in the eastern Democratic Republic of Congo, 2 percent mentioned justice in their priorities, and 85 percent believed it is important to hold accountable those responsible for the violence.[28] In northern Uganda, justice was mentioned as a priority by 3 percent of the population; however, 70 percent maintain that it is important to hold accountable those responsible for the violence.[29] These findings highlight that while peace, security, and basic needs may be perceived as priorities, accountability is nevertheless important to those who experienced conflict. In CAR, when asked why accountability was important, the respondents provided the following reasons: it was owed to the victims (50%), victims must be compensated (48%), justice must be done (17%), and those responsible must be punished (7%).

The alleged crimes for which perpetrators should be held accountable were defined broadly. Nearly all respondents mentioned the killings and murder (91%), and over half mentioned theft, destruction (66%), and rape and sexual violence (52%). Fewer mentioned displacement (15%), forced recruitment of children (8%) and other crimes. Responses were similar across prefectures, except for rape and sexual violence, which were mentioned by 63 percent of respondents in both Bangui and Ombella M'Poko, but less frequently in Lobaye (49%), Ouham Pende (49%), and even less frequently in Ouham (28%).

28   Vinck P, Pham PN, Baldo S, Shigekane R, *Living with Fear: A Population-Based Survey on Attitudes about Peace, Justice and Social Reconstruction in Eastern Congo.* Human Rights Center, University of California, Berkeley; Payson Center for International Development, Tulane University; International Center for Transitional Justice, New York, 2008.

29   Pham PN, Vinck P, Stover E, Moss A, Wierda M, *When the War Ends: A Population-Based Survey on Attitudes about Peace, Justice and Social Reconstruction in Northern Uganda.* Human Rights Center, University of California, Berkeley; Payson Center for International Development, Tulane University; International Center for Transitional Justice, New York, 2007.

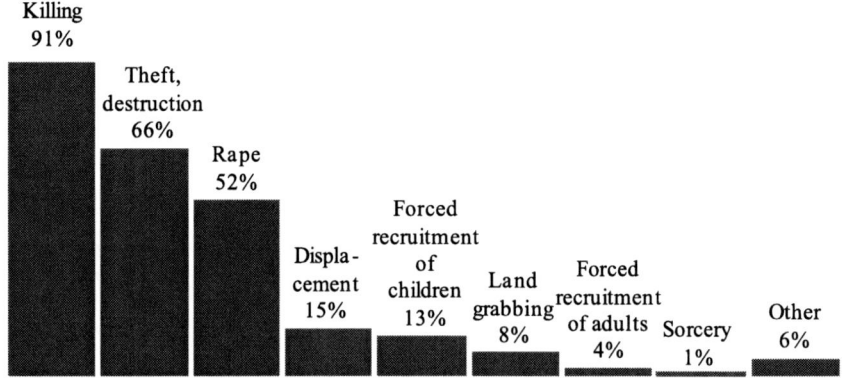

FIGURE 18: CRIMES AND ACCOUNTABILITY

Respondents were further asked who, in their opinion, should be held accountable. They identified a variety of actors reflecting the complex and varied nature of the conflicts in CAR. As with all previous questions in this survey, the questions were open-ended with no response option provided to the respondents; this permits respondents to provide any, and as many, responses as they want. Overall, most respondents pointed to members of the current or previous government: 39 percent said former president Ange-Félix Patassé should be held accountable, while current president François Bozizé was mentioned by 33 percent. Rebel groups, in general with no attribution to a specific name, were mentioned by 20 percent of the respondents, and the current government by 15 percent. There were important differences across prefectures, with the former president mentioned less frequently in the northern prefectures of Ouham and Ouham Pende, while the current president is most frequently mentioned in Ouham Pende. This reflects the increased manipulation of tribalism and regionalism for political gains.[30]

Although the military has allegedly been involved in many crimes, few respondents mentioned the presidential / republican guard (GP/GR) and the Central African Armed Forces (FACA). This possibly means that respondents believe it is the government and politicians who are ultimately responsible for the violence rather than the military who carry out their orders and plans. Jean-Pierre Bemba, currently facing charges of war crimes and crimes against humanity at the International Criminal Court, was mentioned by 13 percent of all the respondents. He was frequently mentioned in Ombella M'Poko (21%), Bangui (19%), and Lobaye (14%).

Next, respondents were asked who, in their opinion, should be in charge of accountability measures. Although many respondents felt the government should be held accountable, nearly half the respondents (47%) also said that the government itself should be in charge of holding accountable

30   International Crisis Group. *Africa Report N°136: Central African Republic: Anatomy of a Phantom State*. Nairobi/Brussels: ICG; 2007.

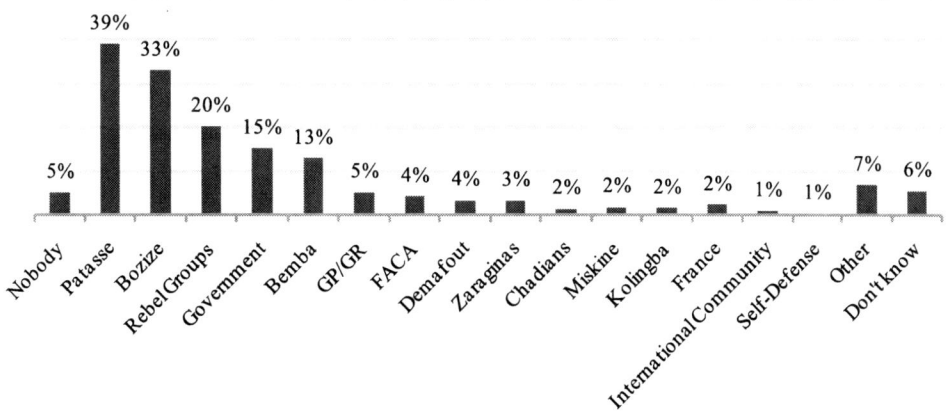

FIGURE 19: WHO SHOULD BE HELD ACCOUNTABLE?

those responsible for the violence. In-depth interviews suggest that this response is associated with the formal judicial system, seen as part of the government. The national judicial system was directly mentioned by 24 percent of the respondents, and the same proportion (24%) said it should be the International Criminal Court.

Since the courts were frequently mentioned as a way to deal with those responsible for the violence, the study further explored the type of judicial measures respondents would like to see implemented in CAR. When given four possible prosecution options, most respondents (52%) favored a trial in CAR by the national court system. The second choice was a trial in CAR by an international court (27%), while 14 percent favored a trial outside of CAR by an international court. Only 7 percent favored no trials at all.

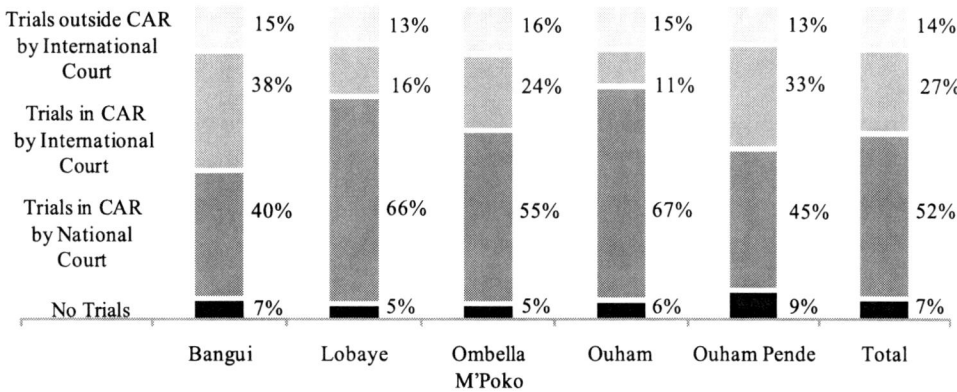

FIGURE 20: TRIAL OPTIONS

Questions relating to the national judicial sector will be explored in the next section. Before turning to questions about justice, however, respondents were asked a more general question about what should happen to those who committed the violence. The most common answers involved sanctions and punishment: 46 percent said they should confront justice and be tried by a court, 27 percent said they should be put in jail, 21 percent said they should be killed, and 19 percent said they should be punished. Fewer said they should be forgiven (5%), ask for forgiveness (5%), and/or tell the truth about their actions (6%).

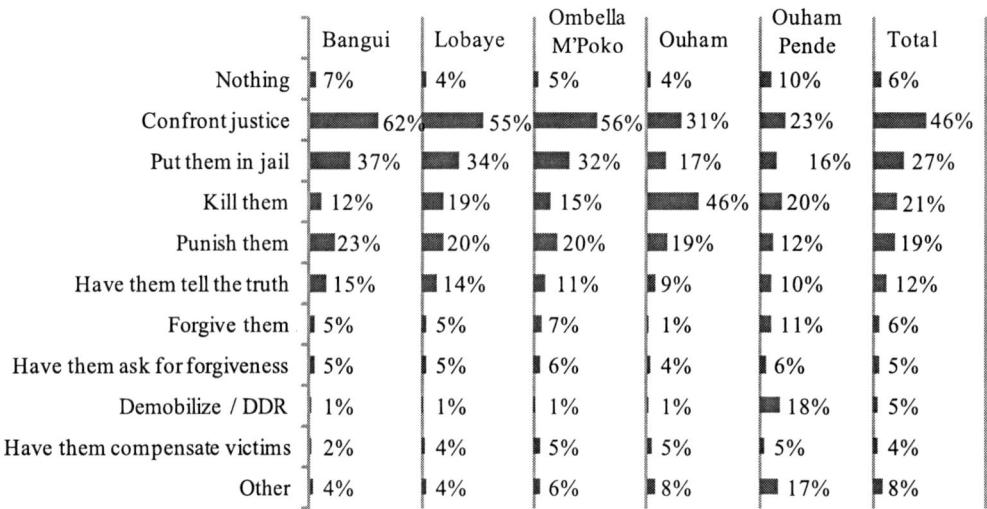

	Bangui	Lobaye	Ombella M'Poko	Ouham	Ouham Pende	Total
Nothing	7%	4%	5%	4%	10%	6%
Confront justice	62%	55%	56%	31%	23%	46%
Put them in jail	37%	34%	32%	17%	16%	27%
Kill them	12%	19%	15%	46%	20%	21%
Punish them	23%	20%	20%	19%	12%	19%
Have them tell the truth	15%	14%	11%	9%	10%	12%
Forgive them	5%	5%	7%	1%	11%	6%
Have them ask for forgiveness	5%	5%	6%	4%	6%	5%
Demobilize / DDR	1%	1%	1%	1%	18%	5%
Have them compensate victims	2%	4%	5%	5%	5%	4%
Other	4%	4%	6%	8%	17%	8%

FIGURE 21: WHAT SHOULD HAPPEN TO THOSE
RESPONSIBLE FOR THE VIOLENCE?

These data suggest that accountability and justice for grave crimes are important for the population in CAR. The survey further suggests that respondents see those measures as important for peace. More than four out of five respondents believe it is impossible to have peace if impunity continues.

THE MEANING OF JUSTICE AND THE JUSTICE SECTOR

As outlined above, the national court system is frequently proposed as the avenue to hold accountable those responsible for the violence committed during the conflicts. Trials in CAR by a national court were the preferred trial option. A series of further questions was designed to assess respondents' perception of the national judicial system. As in northern Uganda, DRC, Rwanda, and Cambodia, respondents in CAR defined justice in broad terms. When asked about the meaning of justice, they most frequently mentioned the strict application of the law (51%), the trial of those who committed crimes (31%), being just or fair (26%), and knowing who is right and who is wrong (17%).

As the discussion on local conflict-resolution showed, few respondents interact with the national judicial system. Rather, most local conflicts are resolved by families themselves, village chiefs, or religious leaders. However, as many as 26 percent said they had had some sort of contact with the formal judicial system over the course of their lives. The type of contact was not discussed. When asked about their knowledge and opinion of the national judicial system, 37 percent of respondents reported having a good or very good knowledge of the system, and 34 percent judged its quality to be good or very good. Inversely, 33 percent judged their knowledge to be poor or very poor, and 36 percent judged the quality of the judicial system to be bad or very bad. When probed further about their opinion, 46 percent of the respondents felt the national judicial system was good and doing its job. However, 39 percent said it was corrupt, 29 percent said justice is only for the rich because it is unfair to the poor, 25 percent said the judges and lawyers were not doing their jobs, and 9 percent said criminals remain unpunished. As many as 32 percent of respondents reported knowing directly of unfair imprisonment, and 28 percent reported knowing of corrupt lawyers and/or judges.

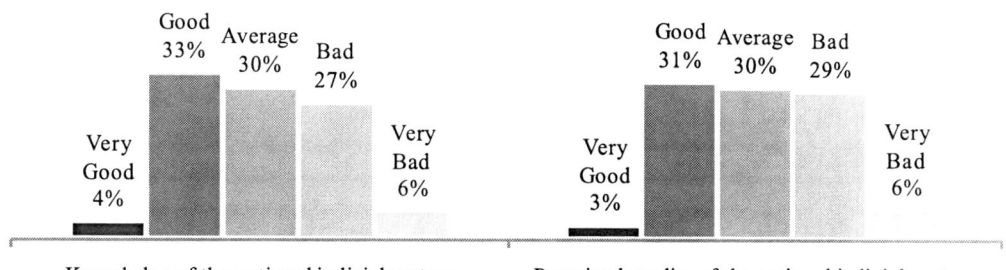

FIGURE 22: KNOWLEDGE AND PERCEPTION OF
THE NATIONAL JUDICIAL SYSTEM

FORGIVENESS AND REVENGE

Despite what appears to be a strong demand for accountability and some form of punishment, a majority of respondents (61%) say it is possible to forgive those responsible for the violence. In fact, 44 percent said they had already forgiven at least some of those responsible. Nevertheless, in order for forgiveness to take place, most respondents said those responsible should first apologize (40%), confess the truth (37%), change their behavior (31%), show remorse (27%), be punished (16%), or compensate the victims for their losses (12%). As the range of responses illustrates, forgiveness does not come easily. While many respondents said it is possible to forgive and some report already having forgiven at least some of the perpetrators, they also report frequently having feelings of hatred for those who committed the violence (57%). Over one in four respondents (27%) indicated they would seek revenge if given the opportunity. This illustrates the complex relationship among accountability, forgiveness, and desire for revenge. They are neither mutually exclusive nor collectively exhaustive.

The International Criminal Court

At the time of the survey, the ICC was just beginning its outreach activities in the interior of the country.[31] The Court had concentrated its activities on the capital, Bangui, and few outreach activities had been conducted in the prefectures of Lobaye and Ombella M'Poko. Overall, one third of respondents

---

31 An in-depth discussion and analysis of results about the ICC is discussed in a forthcoming article: Vinck P, Pham PN. *Outreach Evaluation: The International Criminal Court in the Central African Republic* (forthcoming).

reported having heard about the ICC. Awareness was highest in Bangui (63%) probably because of better access to media, higher levels of education, and outreach by the Court. In Ombella M'Poko and Lobaye, 35 percent and 24 percent of the respondents respectively had heard about the ICC.[32] The high level of awareness in Ombella M'Poko may be explained by a relatively better access to media (especially in the areas bordering Bangui), as well as an interest in the proceedings against Bemba, allegedly responsible for violence that took place in the prefecture. Not surprisingly, given the nature of the outreach activities and the scope of the case currently considered by the ICC, awareness about the ICC was lowest in Ouham Pende (11%) and Ouham (7%). The two prefectures have poor access to media, have not been targeted for outreach, and are experiencing ongoing conflict.

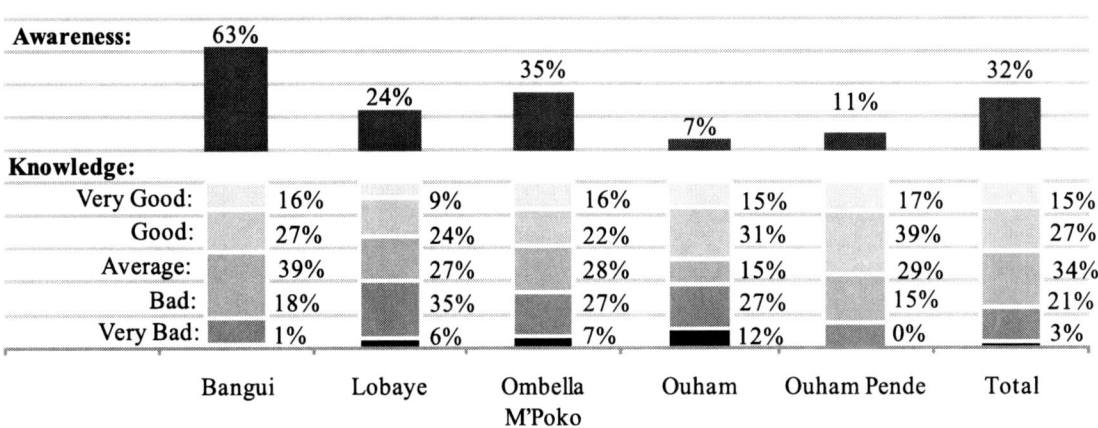

FIGURE 23: KNOWLEDGE AND AWARENESS ABOUT THE ICC

Respondents who indicated having heard about the ICC were asked a series of follow-up questions to judge their knowledge and perception of the court. *The following results are only among those who indicated having heard about the ICC.*

Respondents who had heard about the ICC were asked to rate their knowledge of the court. About two out of five respondents (42%) ranked their knowledge as good or very good, 34 percent ranked their knowledge as average, and 24 percent ranked it as poor or very poor. In Ouham and Ouham Pende, the proportion of respondents ranking their knowledge as good or very good is above 50 percent, which may be due to the fact that few have heard about the ICC and those who did are likely to have a strong interest in learning more about it.

Radio was the most frequent source of information about the ICC: 90 percent mentioned it among their main sources, far more frequently than friends and community (14%), newspapers (12%), or the television (12%). Television and newspapers, however, were almost exclusively mentioned in Bangui,

---

32   In comparison, awareness about the ICC in northern Uganda increased from 25% in 2005 to 60% in 2007. In eastern Democratic Republic of the Congo, 28% of the population had heard about the ICC in 2007. See Vinck et al. and Pham et al. op cited.

while in the other prefectures "friends and community" played a more important role. This is consistent with the more general data on access to mass media.

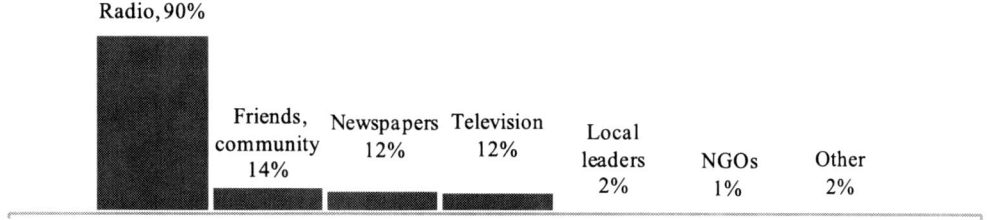

FIGURE 24: ICC – SOURCES OF INFORMATION

Less than 2 percent of those interviewed reported having participated in a meeting about the ICC, the majority of them (77%) having participated in only one meeting. However, more than half of those who had heard about the ICC reported talking at least occasionally about it with friends or neighbors (57%), and 51 percent indicated actively looking for information about the Court.

Two objectives of the ICC's outreach activities are to (1) raise awareness among affected communities regarding the role, mandate, functioning, and activities of the ICC, and (2) ensure the media has rapid access to accurate information regarding judicial proceedings and ICC news for further dissemination to the general public in CAR. Several questions were designed to evaluate respondents' knowledge about the ICC. With regard to the creation of the Court, about half the respondents (47%) believed the ICC was established by the international community, while others believed it had been established by the European community (23%), the U.S. (8%), or CAR (5%). Some were able to identify its date of creation: 23 percent said 2002 and 8 percent said 1998. A larger majority knew where the Court itself was located: 61 percent indicated the Hague or the Netherlands. About the same proportion (65%) knew the Court had offices in CAR, but among them, just 38 percent reported knowing how to access it.

With regard to misinformation, overall few respondents believed the court has been created to investigate crimes committed in CAR only (16% believed so) or in Africa only (22%). However, two-thirds (65%) of those who had heard about the ICC believed the court could investigate crimes committed before 2002. (In fact, the ICC can only investigate crimes committed after July 1, 2002, which means that crimes committed prior to that date in CAR are excluded from the jurisdiction of the Court.)

Awareness and knowledge about the court is associated with the investigation into serious crimes committed in CAR. When asked about who is currently in detention, 80 percent of those who had heard about the ICC were able to identify Jean-Pierre Bemba. Bemba has indeed been charged with three counts of war crimes and two counts of crimes against humanity, all allegedly committed in CAR. A minority of the respondents was able to identify Lubanga (3%), Katanga (2%) or Ngudjolo Chui (1%) who are in detention for crimes allegedly committed in the Democratic Republic of Congo. However, a larger percentage (10%) mistakenly mentioned Charles Taylor, who is on trial at the Special Court of Sierra Leone.

When asked which countries are being investigated by the ICC, respondents accurately mentioned CAR (64%), the DRC (59%), Sudan (35%), and/or Uganda (12%). However, 30 percent also mentioned other countries, and only 5 percent were able to provide four correct answers (i.e., name all four situations). Finally, when asked about individuals who were subject to an arrest warrant, Bashir was most frequently mentioned (39%); followed by Bemba (31%), who is already under arrest; and Kony (16%). However, 21 percent also inaccurately believed an arrest warrant had been issued for CAR's former President Ange-Félix Patassé.[33]

Overall perceptions of the Court are positive. Nearly all respondents who had heard about the ICC believe it is important (95%) because there is a need for justice (51%), because those responsible must be punished (20%), to compensate the victims (10%) or for other reasons. Most (91%) also believe the ICC will have an impact in CAR. Those who believe so most frequently said the ICC would bring justice (27%), help prevent future crimes (20%), help establish the truth about what happened (19%), punish those responsible (14%), help victims (9%), and bring peace (8%). Most respondents (90%) further found the ICC to be just and neutral. Among those who did not believe the ICC to be neutral (10%), respondents generally felt the ICC was working with the government (34%), and that it is after only one group (18%).

The positive perception about the ICC likely explains why most respondents (92%) would be willing to participate in ICC-related activities if possible. Most believed it is indeed possible for victims to participate in ICC proceedings (91%). Most of those willing to participate wanted to provide testimony (80%), participate as a victim (16%), or in other capacities (4%).

Measures for Victims

To understand what affected populations may expect, if anything, from accountability and justice measures, we asked a general question about what should be done for the victims of the conflicts in CAR. The most frequent answers were related to reparation and/or restitution for their losses: 60 percent suggested that victims should be restituted what they have lost as a result of the conflicts, 34 percent said they should receive money, 33 percent said they should receive individual compensation (unspecified), and 25 percent said they should receive services such as health care and education. Fewer respondents mentioned accountability and justice as measures that should be taken for victims: 12 percent said those responsible should be punished, and 10 percent said their suffering should be acknowledged. This, however, does not mean that justice is not important to the victims, as we will see in the next sections. Rather, it points to the wide range of needs expressed by the respondents.

While the question of what should be done for victims was asked in general terms, it is important to note that 65 percent of the population defined themselves as victims. This occurs most frequently in the northern prefectures, Ouham (78%) and Ouham Pende (92%). Respondents provided several

---

33 Ange-Félix Patassé invited Bemba and his MLC troops to help put down a coup in 2002. Crimes alledgedly committed by Bemba's troops during that period are investigated by the ICC.

rationales as to why they considered themselves as victims. They most often reported having lived in conflict-affected areas during periods of violence (59%); having property, animals or land stolen or destroyed (29%); having lost family members (28%); and having directly experienced physical violence (25%). The responses are consistent with data on exposure to violence reported in this study.

More generally, when asked who the victims of the conflicts are, a majority of respondents (75%) identified the whole civilian population, while many also identified specific groups including women (54%), children (46%), and the elderly (25%).

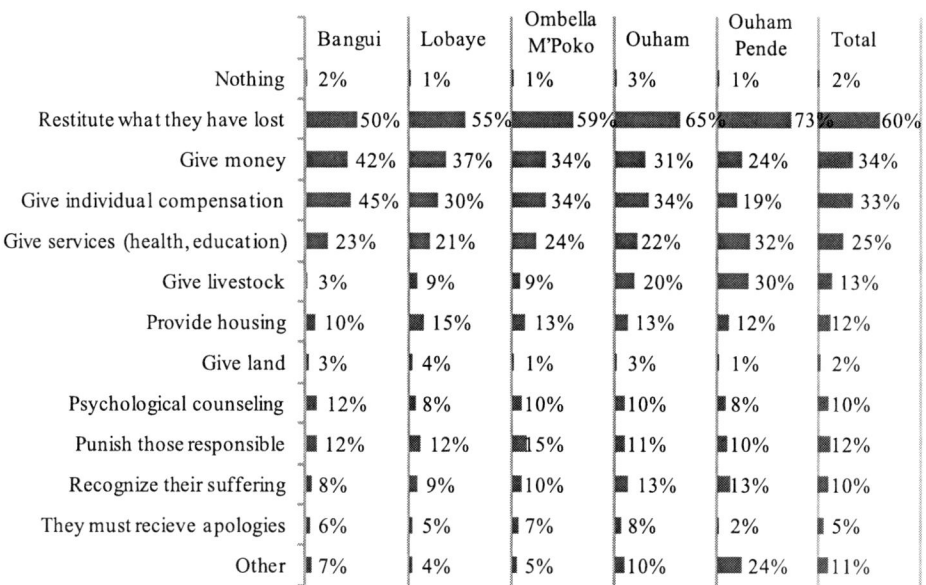

	Bangui	Lobaye	Ombella M'Poko	Ouham	Ouham Pende	Total
Nothing	2%	1%	1%	3%	1%	2%
Restitute what they have lost	50%	55%	59%	65%	73%	60%
Give money	42%	37%	34%	31%	24%	34%
Give individual compensation	45%	30%	34%	34%	19%	33%
Give services (health, education)	23%	21%	24%	22%	32%	25%
Give livestock	3%	9%	9%	20%	30%	13%
Provide housing	10%	15%	13%	13%	12%	12%
Give land	3%	4%	1%	3%	1%	2%
Psychological counseling	12%	8%	10%	10%	8%	10%
Punish those responsible	12%	12%	5%	11%	10%	12%
Recognize their suffering	8%	9%	10%	13%	13%	10%
They must recieve apologies	6%	5%	7%	8%	2%	5%
Other	7%	4%	5%	10%	24%	11%

FIGURE 25: MEASURES FOR VICTIMS

REPARATIONS

When asked what should be done for victims in the previous section, interviewers made no reference to reparations, justice, or accountability. However, the general question was followed by a series of questions on reparations, defined as the ensemble of measures that can be taken for victims. Furthermore, when asked specifically about the importance of providing reparations, most respondents (97%) reported it was important. They further explained that reparation was important because it would help victims recover from their losses (54%), because victims are poor and need the assistance (34%), because it would help victims mentally to forget about what happened (30%), because it would serve as recognition of their suffering (28%), and that it would help bring peace (23%).

Then, respondents were asked again what should be done for victims but with a specific reference to reparations. Responses were somewhat similar to the more general question regarding what should be done for victims: 54 percent said they should be restituted what they have lost, 41 percent said to give money, 30 percent said to give individual compensation, and 26 percent mentioned improving services including health care and education.

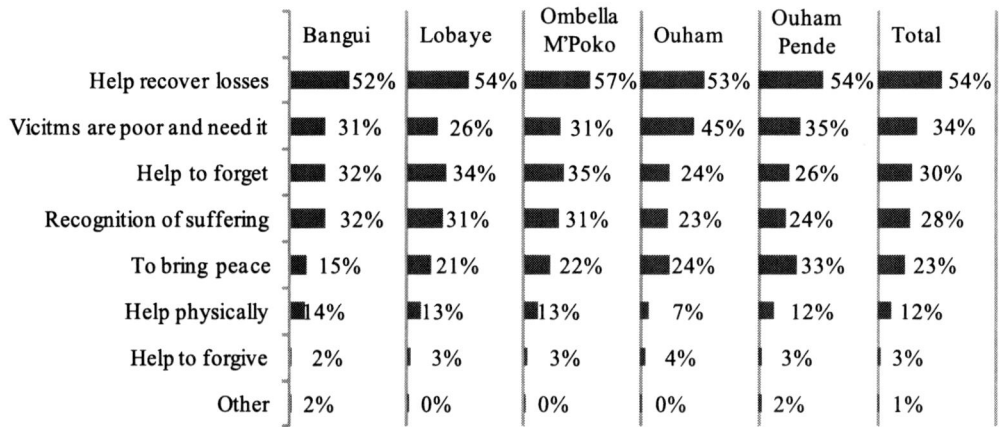

	Bangui	Lobaye	Ombella M'Poko	Ouham	Ouham Pende	Total
Help recover losses	52%	54%	57%	53%	54%	54%
Vicitms are poor and need it	31%	26%	31%	45%	35%	34%
Help to forget	32%	34%	35%	24%	26%	30%
Recognition of suffering	32%	31%	31%	23%	24%	28%
To bring peace	15%	21%	22%	24%	33%	23%
Help physically	14%	13%	13%	7%	12%	12%
Help to forgive	2%	3%	3%	4%	3%	3%
Other	2%	0%	0%	0%	2%	1%

FIGURE 26: WHY IS IT IMPORTANT TO PROVIDE REPARATIONS?

Respondents said most frequently that such reparations should be provided at both the individual and community levels (43%), while 37 percent said it should be at the community level, and 20 percent said it should be at the individual level. However, about half the respondents (47%) said they would accept only community-level reparations. More were willing to accept only symbolic reparations (56%), but only 13 percent were willing to accept no reparations at all.

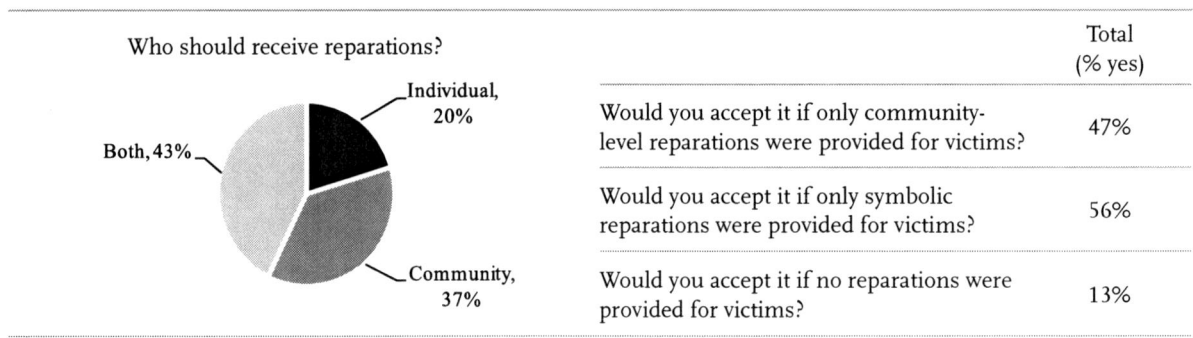

FIGURE 27: REPARATIONS

A majority of respondents (79%) attached importance to the person or organization who should pay for the reparations. They generally said it should be the government (35%) or the international community (31%). Some mentioned the International Criminal Court (9%), the president (7%), and those responsible for the violence themselves (6%).

	Bangui	Lobaye	Ombella M'Poko	Ouham	Ouham Pende	Total
Government	30%	46%	36%	39%	31%	
International community	35%	24%	27%	28%	35%	
ICC	15%	5%	11%	5%	6%	
President	2%	7%	6%	13%	11%	
Those responsible	7%	7%	9%	7%	1%	
Local community	6%	5%	5%	3%	2%	
Patasse	1%	2%	1%	1%	4%	
Other	5%	2%	3%	4%	6%	
Don't know	1%	2%	3%	1%	4%	

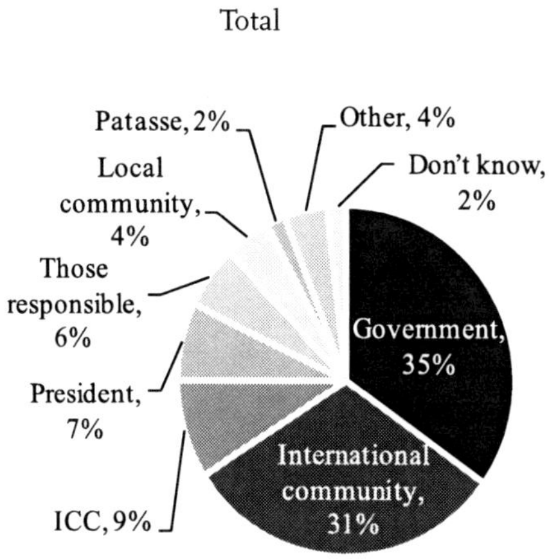

FIGURE 28: WHO SHOULD PAY FOR REPARATIONS?

Truth-Seeking and Memorialization

As shown in our other research in Cambodia, DRC, Iraq, and northern Uganda, it is important for civilians affected by violence to know what happened during the conflict and why. In CAR, 89 percent of respondents said it is important to know what happened. They most frequently say it is important because the truth must be known (58%), to understand why the conflicts and violence happened (42%), and to know who is responsible (35%).

A majority of the population (80%) was willing to talk openly and publicly about what they or their family have experienced. Most of them were willing to do so because they felt they owed it to themselves (37%), because it was their duty (26%), or so those responsible would be known and identified (25%). Those who said they were not willing to talk openly about their experience most frequently said it was because they were afraid of reprisals (38%), because it was not their role (29%), because they did not want to remember the past (13%), or because they had nothing to say (10%).

While establishing the truth about what happened is a common demand, there is much debate on how this can best be achieved, and on the role of memorialization. This study did not discuss such processes, but respondents were nevertheless asked whether they believed memorials were important. A majority answered positively (74%). Among them, they generally said memorials were important so the past could not be easily forgotten (55%), memorials would pay respect to the victims (39%), educate the youth (32%), provide recognition of the violence (16%), and help explain what happened (12%).

Among those who did not believe memorials were important (26%), they generally felt that the community should forget (44%) and that it would bring back bad memories (44%). About one in four (26%) also said such memorials would be useless because the past is already known.

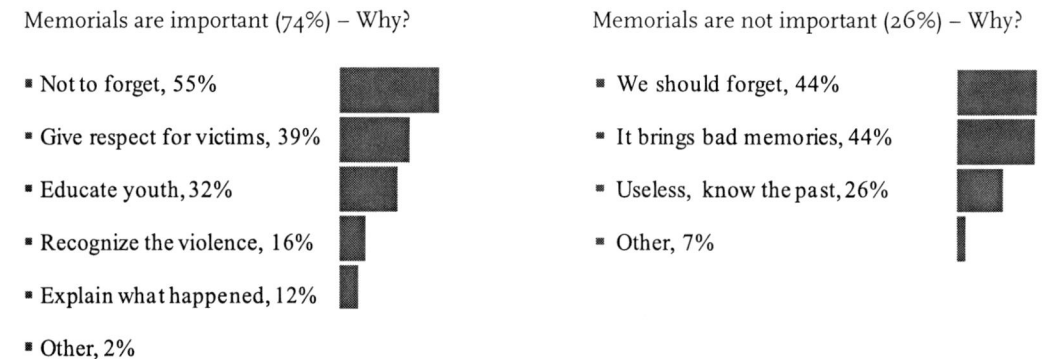

Memorials are important (74%) – Why?

- Not to forget, 55%
- Give respect for victims, 39%
- Educate youth, 32%
- Recognize the violence, 16%
- Explain what happened, 12%
- Other, 2%

Memorials are not important (26%) – Why?

- We should forget, 44%
- It brings bad memories, 44%
- Useless, know the past, 26%
- Other, 7%

FIGURE 29: MEMORIALS

CONCLUSIONS & RECOMMENDATIONS

THESE KEY SURVEY RESULTS should be instructive to the Government of the Central African Republic, nongovernmental organizations, and other agencies as they develop policies to address the legacy of armed conflict in CAR. They are also a reminder that consulting the population and deepening our understanding of war-affected communities is essential to build a lasting peace.

The key recommendations to emerge from this study are:

To the CAR Government and Armed Groups:

- Work together to implement the goals of the Inclusive Political Dialogue, including the effective disarmament, demobilization, and reintegration of combatants back into society, and hold free and fair presidential elections. The citizens of CAR view combatant reintegration programs and elections as integral steps for building a lasting peace.

- Stop preying on the population and collecting illegal taxes at road blocks. These instill fear among the population, which hinders their ability to carry on with their daily lives.

To the CAR Government:

- Reform the security sector and remove perpetrators of serious crimes from their positions. The police and *gendarmes* must be trained and supported to fulfill their mandate of protecting—not preying on—civilians.

- Bring those responsible for violations of human rights and international humanitarian law to justice. The government should support the judiciary to ensure that courts can operate independently and fairly. This will help raise public confidence in the judiciary and support the rule of law.

- Prioritize the provision of basic services including education, health care, and transportation (e.g., road network).

To the Civil Society and the International Community:

- Pressure the government, political parties, and armed groups to ensure that elections and DDR processes are effectively implemented in a transparent, free, and fair manner.

- Provide sufficient financial and technical support to the electoral process to guarantee free and fair elections and ensure a peaceful transition.

- Work with the government to rebuild infrastructure and services and uphold the rule of law. The focus on humanitarian needs in the north should not prevent investment to address structural and chronic poverty in all of CAR. Respondents identified peace, employment, and basic services as priorities. If any of these are neglected, political and physical stability will be hard to establish and sustain.

- Engage with the population to address domestic violence and other forms of violence at the community level.

- Continue to document violations of human rights and international humanitarian law and press for accountability. The international community should continue to support civil society in its efforts to document human rights abuses and assist victims. The international community should also maintain a UN peacekeeping mission in CAR for the foreseeable future. Its presence will help guarantee a certain level of stability and allow for the completion of DDR, elections, and reform of the security sector.

- Work to develop a regional security strategy to address cross-border issues and lawless border zones.

To the International Criminal Court:

- Continue and increase public information and outreach activities especially in the interior of the country. The proportion of respondents who are aware of the ICC was relatively high, but there is still a great need to target groups with little or no access to media.

- Reconsider holding *in situ* proceedings in CAR, security condition permitting. The survey found strong support for local trials.

- Broaden the scope of investigations to include serious crimes committed throughout the country, especially in the north.

- Work with national institutions to ensure the investigation contributes to establishing a historical record of the events in CAR.

AUTHORS AND ACKNOWLEDGEMENT

Phuong Pham and Patrick Vinck led the design of the survey and data collection in the Central African Republic, and wrote this report.

PATRICK VINCK is Director of the Initiative for Vulnerable Populations at UC Berkeley's Human Rights Center, Visiting Associate Professor at UC Berkeley, and Adjunct Associate Professor at Tulane University's Payson Center for International Development.

PHUONG PHAM is Director of Research at UC Berkeley's Human Rights Center, Visiting Associate Professor at UC Berkeley, and Adjunct Associate Professor at Tulane University's Payson Center for International Development.

This research would not have been possible without the voluntary participation of the respondents. We are grateful to the interviewers who have conducted an outstanding work in difficult conditions, and to all the individuals and organizations who have helped us along the way. For confidentiality reasons, individual acknowledgements will not be listed here. However, this report would not have been possible without their support.

At the Human Rights Center, Mobile Technology Specialist Neil Hendrick contributed to the field supervision and programming of the PDAs for data collection. Camille Crittenden and Liza Jimenez navigated the administrative hurdles and production and editing of the report. Michelle Arevalo-Carpenter contributed to the background research. Austin McKinley provided the original illustration on the cover. Nicole Hayward designed the report.

This survey was conducted by the Initiative for Vulnerable Populations, a project of UC Berkeley's Human Rights Center.

The **INITIATIVE FOR VULNERABLE POPULATIONS** conducts research in countries experiencing serious violations of human rights and international humanitarian law. Using empirical research methods to give voice to survivors of mass violence, the Initiative aims to ensure that the needs of survivors are recognized and acted on by governments, UN agencies, and non-governmental organizations.

The **HUMAN RIGHTS CENTER** promotes human rights and international justice worldwide and trains the next generation of human rights researchers and advocates. More information about our projects can be found at http://hrc.berkeley.edu.

This report was made possible by grants from the John D. and Catherine T. MacArthur Foundation and Humanity United. The information provided and views expressed in this publication do not necessarily reflect the views of these funding agencies.

Other reports in this series include:

Pham PN, Vinck P, Balthazard M, Hean S, Stover E (2009), *So We Will Never Forget: A Population-Based Survey on Attitudes about Social Reconstruction and the Extraordinary Chambers in the Courts of Cambodia.* Human Rights Center, University of California, Berkeley.

Vinck P, Pham PN, Baldo S, Shigekane R (2008), *Living with Fear: A Population-Based Survey on Attitudes about Peace, Justice and Social Reconstruction in Eastern Congo.* Human Rights Center, University of California, Berkeley; Payson Center for International Development, Tulane University; International Center for Transitional Justice, New York.

Pham PN, Vinck P, Stover E, Moss A, Wierda M (2007), *When the War Ends. A Population-Based Survey on Attitudes about Peace, Justice and Social Reconstruction in Northern Uganda.* Human Rights Center, University of California, Berkeley; Payson Center for International Development, Tulane University; International Center for Transitional Justice, New York.

Pham PN, Vinck P, Wierda M, Stover E, di Giovanni A. (July 2005), *Forgotten Voices: A Population-Based Survey of Attitudes about Peace and Justice in Northern Uganda.* International Center for Transitional Justice and the Human Rights Center, University of California, Berkeley.

To download these and other reports, visit http://hrc.berkeley.edu/publications.

Cover illustration by Austin McKinley, 2010.

CPSIA information can be obtained at www.ICGtesting.com
Printed in the USA
LVOW020131211111

255514LV00018B/1/P